African American Achievers in Science, Medicine, and Technology

A Resource Book for Young Learners, Parents, Teachers, and Librarians

By

Wina Marché

ISBN: 1-4107-2895-1 (e-book)
ISBN: 1-4107-2894-3 (Paperback)
ISBN: 1-4140-0582-2 (Dust Jacket)

Library of Congress Control Number: 2003092010

.This book is printed on acid free paper.

Printed in the United States of America
Bloomington, IN

1stBooks - rev. 08/29/03

Table of Contents

iv

PART ELEVEN: LATER INVENTORS (Continued)

PART TWELVE: MODERN INVENTORS

PART TWELVE: MODERN INVENTORS (Continued)

Acknowledgments

First, I thank the historians, authors, editors, and reporters who write about African Americans achievers in science, medicine, and technology.

Equally important are the following individuals who allowed me to test ideas with them.; Mrs. Edna Berry, Mrs. Elsie McParker Bingham, Mrs. Elsie Brooks, Atty. Laura Graham of the Detroit Fair Housing Center, Mrs. Barbara Glenn, Dr. Betty Gray, Mrs. Alma Greer, Mrs. Johnnye Grimmett, Mrs. Amy Jackson, Mrs. Jacqueline G. Johnson, Dr. Darnell Lassister, Dr. H. Michael Lemmons, Ms. Michele Massey, Mrs. Dorothy Patterson, Mrs. Alberta Price, Mr. Elmer Price, Ms. Carla Reczek, Dr. Mary Session, Mrs. Gwendolyn Smith, Mrs. Sally Sullivan, Ms. Darlene Thomas, Mr. Errol Thomas, Dr. Mabon Thomas, Mrs. Patricia Thomas, Ms. Gail Twitty, Mrs. Barbara Twyman, Atty. Beverly Anthony Walker, Mrs. Margaret Ward, Mr. Carlos Watts, and Ms. Johnella Wells. I can't thank them enough.

Finally, thanks to the staff of the Detroit Public Library system, especially the Main Branch, the U.S. Great Lakes Patent and Trademark Center, and the Parkman Branch. The librarians were gracious, helpful, and seemed happy to share information.

Introduction

Perhaps, you can name many African American achievers in sports and entertainment but not many in other fields. This book will help you fill that void in science, medicine, and technology.

I became aware of the need for this type of information after reading a local newspaper story about African Americans in high school. I don't remember the point the story (a full page) attempted to make. However, it was clear that some of the young learners interviewed thought that their peers who were studying and trying to achieve were "acting White"!

Of course I didn't believe the story and did my own research/survey. Indeed, this belief seemed to be widespread! I realized that young African Americans who feel this way know very little about African American achievers in America's history. Not only young learners, but most Americans don't know much about African American achievers.

To share information is this mission. So, young learners, parents, teachers, and librarians meet one hundred-fifty African American achievers in science, medicine, and technology. Their lives have been researched and recorded by historians, reporters, editors, and writers. I present them to you in poems.

The idea of poetry as a medium was inspired by an incident at a community meeting. During the "meet, greet, and eat" part of the meeting, a young woman spotted me in the crowd. She waved, ran across the room, and grabbed me in a "bear hug". She said that I had been her third grade auditorium teacher and that she was very shy in those days. She recalled, despite her shyness, I insisted she go on stage and recite a poem using the microphone.

Suddenly, as if reliving the third grade on stage experience, she burst (*and I do mean burst, like a broadway star delivering a show stopper*) into the recitation of a poem about mice. It "brought down the house" with laughter! Someone said, "She's not shy anymore!" After twenty-five years she remembered that poem!

Hopefully you will enjoy meeting the achievers and gathering more information from the sources listed. Maybe **you** will read one of the poems and remember it twenty-five years from today!

Wina Marché
Detroit, Michigan
February, 2003

PART ONE

EARLY INNOVATORS

Dr. Solomon Carter Fuller

Born in Monrovia, Liberia   (1872-1953)
Physician, Psychiatrist, Neurologist, Pathologist;
First Black to Practice Psychiatry in the U.S.
Boston Health Center Named for Him

Solomon Carter Fuller's
 story begins two hundred years
 ago, with his grandfather,
 John Lewis Fuller, who
left the U.S. for Africa, -
 Monrovia, Liberia to be exact,
 to allay his family's fears.

He bought his and his wife's freedom,
 but they still were in harm's way.
Slave owners thought folk like them
 troublemakers and threats to slavery.
So, a group helped free Black people
 leave the harm they faced everyday.

Let's pick up the story later.
 Some sixty years, in 1889.
John Lewis Fuller's grandson,
 Solomon C. Fuller arrives,

age seventeen, in the U.S.
   education here, he thinks is fine.

Within four years, his first degree
   was earned; next came his dream,
   medicine at Boston U.
There he earned the title Doctor;
   then internship at the hospital
   in the real world from academe.

There in the hospital for the insane
   Dr. Fuller began his career –
   research in brain diseases.
He became an authority
   on several mental illnesses,
   as a researcher and pioneer.

Research and study filled his days.
   There was little balance in his life.
There were exciting adventures
   like meeting Sigmund Freud
   and leaders in psychiatry.
Balance came when he met his wife.

Meta Vaux Warrick, an artist
   studying at Westborough State

College, became his wife in

year 1909 and changed his life.

His hobby of portrait prints was

her idea. His work was top rate.

Dr. Fuller's work in medicine,

his writings, his contributions

to psychiatry and mental illness;

his work as a neurologist;

as a pathologist were the bases

to build on for medical solutions.

Sources

Hayden, Robert C. *II African American Doctors*. (New York: Twenty-First Books, 1976), p. 18-35.

McKissack, Patricia and McKissack, Frederick. *African American Scientists*. (Brookfield, Connecticut, Millbrook Press, 1994), 60.

Morais, Herbert Monfort. *The History of the Negro in Medicine*. (New York: Publishers Co., 1967), p. 104-105.

Sammons, Vivian Ovelton. *Blacks in Science and Medicine*. (New York: Hemisphere Publishing Co., 1990), p. 93.

Wina Marché

Dr. George Cleveland Hall

(1864-1930) Ypsilanti, Michigan
Bennett College of Medicine Chicago 1888
Physician; Surgeon; Gynecologist

Hall worked with Dr. Daniel Hale
    Williams. Helped him prevail
in organizing Provident Hospital of Chicago.
    Helped medicine in Chicago grow
with first post graduate class.
    Helped establish infirmaries en masse
throughout cities of our nation's
    south, for better health care collaborations.

Sources

Cox, Clinton. Haskins, Jim, general editor. *African American Healers*.
    (New York: John Wiley & Sons, Inc., 2000), p. 70-72.
Jet. February 24, 1955. p. 10.
Kaufman, Martin, Galishoff, et al, editors. 2 vols. *Dictionary of American Medical Biography*. (Westport, CT.: Greenwood Press, 1984), p. 316-317.
Morais, Herbert M. *The History of the Negro in Medicine*. (New York: Publishers Company, Inc., 1968), p. 74, 75, 77-78.

Dr. Percy Lavon Julian

Montgomery, Alabama 1899-1975
PhD Chemistry University of Vienna (Vienna, Austria) – 1931
Scientist, Soybean Chemist, Synthesis of Cortisone

With pain in her knee
   an elder would would say,
   "Arthur is whipping me!"
   On any given day
   arthritis was refrained
   before Julian attained
   cortisone success
   with a synthesizing process.

Percy's high school classes were a breeze.
His dream was DePauw University.
He won a scholarship there with ease.
You can guess there was some adversity.
Besides there being no other Blacks,
   he had some academic setbacks.

DePauw put him two years behind!
He carried a double class load –
   the usual college freshman grind
   plus a high school class load.

7

He passed them all with flying colors
    surpassing 159 others!

160 graduates and Percy was the first!
His family was proud he was the lead!
That ancestral yearning, a burning thirst-
    a slave ancestor attacked for learning to read!
Their modern yearnings were tied to college.
Five siblings attained college knowledge.

Back to Percy and graduate school blocks,
    the future looked bleak and rather stark,
    more ways to construct doors with locks.
Black college teaching brightened the dark.
A Masters degree from Harvard U.
    soothed all feelings dark, gray or blue.

More closed doors, more dreams died.
Percy found each opened door was better
    than the opportunities closed doors denied.
With his PhD. this was true to the letter.
From Vienna, Austria, a foreign land,
    Ernest Spaeth extended a helping hand.

Spaeth was an expert in chemical synthesis.
Chemical synthesis in language, simply stated

means something in nature gets an analysis
so chemists can find something related
to copy nature at a cheaper price.
Julian accomplished this more than twice.

His research helped ease human pain
in a swollen limb or in joint disease.
Cortisone is now cheaper and easy to obtain
it was a major medicine for pain ease.
Before Dr. Julian it was very expensive.
Its production with ox liver was extensive.

Looking for hormones cheaper by the gram
Dr. Julian went to neighboring Mexico
to study the possible use of the wild yam
to see if production costs would be low.
He did research and built a facility there
and with other ventures was a millionaire.

Dr. Percy Julian was a brilliant man.
He had 130 patents to his name.
What a productive 76-year life span;
scientific contributions, vision, and fame!
Many awards and monuments proclaim
what he achieved and what he overcame!

Sources

Aaseng, Nathan. *Black Inventors*. (New York: Facts On File, Inc., 1997), p. 113-124.

Cox, Clinton Jim Haskins, general editor. *African American Healers*. (New York: John Wiley & Sons, Inc. 2000), p. 109-114.

Sullivan, Otha Richard. Jim Haskins, general editor. *African American Inventors*. (New York: John Wiley & Sons, Inc., 1998), p. 95-101.

U.S. Patent Office Microfilm. *Percy Lavon Julian*. No. 2,752,339. Great Lakes June 26, 1956. Patent and Trademark Center. Detroit Public Library. Detroit.

U.S. Patent Office Microfilm. *Percy Lavon* Julian. No. 3,149,132. September, 15, 1964. Lakes Patent and Trademark Center. Detroit Public Library. Detroit.

U.S. Patent Office Microfilm. *Percy Lavon Julian*. No. 3,274,178. September, 20, 1966. Great Lakes Patent and Trademark Center. Detroit Public Library. Detroit.

Dr. Ernest Everett Just

Born Charleston, South Carolina (1883-1941)
Biologist, Zoologist, Physiologist;
PhD in Zoology University Chicago 1916
Major Contributor to the Study of Cells;
Published in U.S., Europe, Japan
Over 60 Research Papers Based Upon
His Cell Research and Discoveries

August 14, 1883
Ernest E. Just came to be.
His fifty-eight year sojourn here
was marked by a brilliant career.

An outstanding student in college
"Magna Cum Laude" was his knowledge.
At Howard U. he showed his mettle;
later the first NAACP Spingarn Medal.

The microscope and the single cell
held secrets he was able to tell.
Dr. Just by 1929
was a researcher near the Rhine.

Because of the Nazi German advance,
Dr. Just moved his research to France;
where later he was a P.O.W.
He returned to the U.S. and Howard U.

Dr. Just brought attention to the cell.
Important information he did foretell.
He added new knowledge to the topic
with theories and research microscopic.

Sources

Haber, Louis. *Black Pioneers of Science and Invention.* (New York: Harcourt Brace & Company, 1970), 161-175.

Sammons, Vivian Ovelton. *Blacks in Science and Medicine.* (New York: Hemisphere Publishing Co., 1990), p. 141.

Sullivan, Otha Richard. *African American Inventors.* New York: John Wiley & Sons, Inc., 1998), p. 81-84.

Yount, Lisa. *Black Scientists.* (New York: Facts on File, 1991), p. 28-40.

Dr. Theodore K. Lawless

(1892-1971) Thibodeaux, Louisiana

Dermatologist; Northwestern School of Medicine; Philanthropist

Talladega College; Harvard University

Nearly 200 years ago

another was deemed to know

much about skin, Papan,

a slave, was his name. – a man,

with "medicine in his hand",

from Africa his native land.

Dr. Lawless had the modern touch.

He too about the skin knew much.

The U. S., Israel (a clinic has his name),

a chapel at Dillard U. has the same.

Many places U.S., Europe, college

contributed to his knowledge

His honors and awards were legion.

They came from many a region.

The doctor's many good deeds

were all ministering to needs.

A medical legend graced this earth;

many knew and appreciated his worth.

Sources

Kaufman, Martin, Galishoff, et al, editors. 2 vols. *Dictionary of American Medical* Biography. (Westport, D.T.: Greenwood Press, 1984), p. 437-438.

Morais, Herbert Montfort. *The History of the Negro in Medicine.* (New York: Publishers Co., 1967), p. 317.

Robinson, Wilhelmena S. *Historical Negro Biographies.* (New York: Publishers Co., 1968), p. 291.

Sammons, Vivian Ovelton. *Blacks in Science and Medicine.* (New York: Hemisphere Publishing Corporation, 1990), p. 148.

Dr. Daisy Hill Northcross

(1881-19??) Montgomery, Alabama
Loyola Medical College 1913
Dr. David C. Northcross – Husband
Co-founders of Mercy Hospital-Detroit

They were a medical team,
    Dr. Daisy and husband, held in esteem .
by their patients and community. She
    was a co-founder of Mercy Hospital. He
had no problem with ladies healing.
    Some men of that era had trouble dealing
with lady doctors. Many years later
    acceptance was hardly any greater.
Dr. Daisy was medical pioneer
    and an innovator, a medical peer.

Sources

Davis, Marianna W. ed. *Contributions of Black Women in America.*
    Columbia, S.C.: Kenday Press, 1982 vol. p. 245.
Ebony. Chicago: Johnson Publishing Co. October 1950. p. 38.

Matney, William. *Who's Who Among Black Americans*. (Lake Forest, Illinois: Educational Communications, Inc., 1985), p. 393.

Sammons, Vivian Ovelton. *Blacks in Science and Medicine*. (New York: Hemisphere Publishing Corporation. 1990.) p. 181-182.

Wright, Dr. Roberta Hughes. *Detroit Memorial Park Cemetery: Evolution of an African American Corporation*. (Southfield Michigan: Charro Book Company, Inc., 1993), p. 15.

Dr. Charles Burleigh Purvis

(1842-1929) Philadelphia, Pennsylvania
Wooster Medical College (Western Reserve Medical College)
1865 – Obstetrics and Gynecology

Young Charles and his siblings
    made eight.
The wealthy, the well-known
    and the great
Leaders against slavery were
    often his parents' guests.
They talked of activities
    and anti-slavery quests.
It is only natural that
    service and causes
Would guide his life
    despite sidetracks and pauses.

Dr. Charles Burleigh
    Purvis' acclaim
With Dr. Alexander T.
    Augusta was common aim,
To teach Blacks medicine
    in the U.S.

17

This they did at Howard U.

and trained the "best".

Howard had financial

trouble in 1873.

Augusta, Purvis, and one other

MD taught classes for free!

The doctors believed in medical care

and the country's need.

Their mission was to help

Howard U. succeed.

Dr. Purvis was known for dedication

and a willingness to act.

His fifty-seven years at Howard U.

had a great impact

On America's medical care

and the Black physician.

He was a role model for medical

activism and tradition.

Sources

Cox, Clinton and Haskins, Jim, general editor. *African American Healers.* (New York: John Wiley & Sons, Inc., 2000), p. 46-50.

Kaufman, Martin, Galishoff, et al, editors. 2 vols. *Dictionary of American Medical Biography*. (Westport, CT: Greenwood Press, 1984), p. 612-613.

Logan, Rayford W., and Winston, Michael Reeds. *Dictionary Of The American Negro Biography*. 1st edition. (New York: Norton, 1983), p. 507-508.

Morais, Herbert M. *The History of the Negro in Medicine*. (New York: Publishers Co., 1968), p. 51-52.

Wina Marché

Dr. Charles H. Turner

Born in Cincinnati, Ohio (1867-1923)
PhD University of Chicago
Biologist; Research Scientist; Teacher; Findings About Ants

His name, a symbol of outreach;
    a scientist seeker of facts;
    a researcher called to teach;
    a man of noble deeds and acts.

An observer of lifestyles
    among spiders, ants, and bees;
    an observer of errors and trials
    when an insect hears and sees.

From insect research he wrote
    and published some forty plus
    papers of international note
    that scientists still read and discuss.

A scientific term bears his name
    "turner's circling" a French term
    based on his ant research fame
    others were able to confirm.

His interests had quite a reach;

> writing children's science stories,

> poetry, civil rights, the call to teach,

> were among his personal glories.

Sources

Carwell, Hattie. *Blacks in Science: Astrophysicist to Zoologist.* (Hicksville, N.Y.: Exposition Press, 1977), p. 24-25.

Hayden, Robert C. *Achievers: African Americans in Science and Technology-7 African American Scientists.* (New York: Twenty-First Century Books, 1992), p. 34-57.

McKissack, Patricia and McKissack, Frederick. *African-American Scientists.* (Brookfield, Connecticut: The Millbrook Press, 1994), p. 73-77.

Sammons, Vivian Ovelton. *Blacks in Science and Medicine.* (New York: Hemisphere Publishing Corporation, 1990), p. 235.

Madame C.J. Walker

(Sarah Breedlove McWilliams Walker)

(1867-1919) Delta, Louisiana Cotton Plantation
Inventor of Hair Grower-Entrepreneur; Philanthropist; Innovator

Madame Walker's early life
*   was about struggle, sadness, strife.*
Madame Walker's story is about success,
*   potential, persistence, progress;*
*   having less, needing more,*
*   sharing, teaching, opening another door!*

Eighteen sixty-seven was the year
    the Breedloves' only holiday cheer
    came December, the twenty-third day,
    with Christmas just two days away.
    her name was Sarah, a precious one.
There were no other gifts, none.

Sarah was an orphan seven years later.
Hard times and poverty were even greater.
They lost their one-room home – no money.
Their life was the other side of sunny.
Sarah and sister moved to another state.
Separation seemed to be their fate.

Marriage for each was the open door
    that lead to a life better than before.
McWilliams was Sarah's new name.
She liked the sound of certain acclaim.
Three years later in 1892
    their baby girl's birth was due.

Baby Lelia was their delight
Life for them had reached a new height.
Two years later there was, again, despair.
More sadness for Sarah seemed unfair.
Husband, Moses, died in an accident.
Once again Sarah had cause to lament.

Sarah and baby chose another state.
Life was better, but not all that great.
She joined church, historic St. Paul
    A.M.E., noted for its kindness to all.
Things were better in St. Louis City
Help was given with dignity, not pity.

By the time Lelia needed higher learning
    Sarah had reached a higher level of earning.
Indeed, Leila was to be college educated!
Sarah's ex-slave parents would have been elated!

They wanted Sarah to be the first one,
    but poverty she wasn't able to outrun.

Sarah was always neat and clean in dress
    to promote her laundry business.
But she was concerned about falling hair.
Hers had broken ends and patches, bare.
Other Black ladies felt the same distress
    that existing products did not address.

Sarah tried every type of known hair care.
Nothing seemed to help her thinning hair.
Inventing her own solution was her goal
For growing hair healthy and whole.
The answer came to her in a dream.
Her invention was a hair growing cream.

It was time for a move, an open door.
Moving this time, to Denver, was no chore.
Sister-in-law and four children needed her.
Sarah knew they needed to help each other.
She cooked to finance her work in hair loss.
A Candian born druggist was her new boss.

Sarah worked on her formula at night,
    mixing and testing to get it just right.

She took in laundry two days too.

    that's how her business money grew.

With her home grown marketing skill

    she had many hair cream orders to fill.

Sarah's friend C.J. came to Denver town.

They got married and settled down.

Her new name was easy to say

    Walker, Madame C.J.

That was 1906 and business was growing,

    promoting, Madame C.J. was busy going.

Eventually there were thousands selling

    buying, teaching at her schools, telling,

    their stories of growing more hair.

They were earning money from hair care.

Factories and franchises were on her list.

She gave marketing a "brand new" twist.

While caring for other people's hair

Madame Walker became a millionaire.

For many she provided an open door

    when they had less and needed more.

She gave thousands of dollars to fight

    for Causes to make things right.

Wina Marché

Madame Walker's early life
*   was about struggle, sadness, strife.*
Madame Walker's story is about success,
*   potential, persistence, progress;*
*   needing more, getting more*
*   sharing, teaching, opening another door.*

Sources

Aaseng, Nathan. *Black Inventors*. (New York: Facts on File, Inc., 1997), p. 75-86.

Bundles, A'Lelia Perry. *Madam C.J. Walker, Entrepreneur*. (Philadelphia: Chelsea House Publishers, 1991).

Hine, Darlene Clark. ed. *Black Women in America – An Historical Encyclopedia, Volume II*. (Brooklyn, New York: Carlson Publishing Inc, 1993), p. 1209-1214.

Sullivan, Otha Richard. *African American Inventors*. (New York: John Wiley & Sons, Inc., 1998), p. 70-74.

Dr. Daniel Hale Williams

Born in Hollidaysburg, PA (1856-1931); MD Chicago Medical College (Northwestern Medical School) 1883; Performed the First Successful Surgery on Tissue Around the Heart 1893; Founded Chicago's Provident Hospital 1891; and National Medical Association; Charter Member of the American College of Surgeons

Mister Dan
>was a versatile man;
>a barber, a cobbler, waiter;
>soon to be a medicine man.

Doctor Dan
>was a versatile man;
>student of law, music man;
>then he was a medicine man.

"Dr. Dan,
>Dr. Dan,
>the man has a knife in his chest!"

Dr. Dan had to do what was best.

Dr. Dan's
>plan was surgery to save a life!
>He carefully opened the man's chest.

Medical history tells the rest!

Dr. Dan

was a farsighted medical man;

noble were his medical goals;

leader, founder were his roles.

Let's salute Dr. Dan,

a very versatile man,

a Black medical pioneer,

in a lifesaving career.

Sources

Cox, Clinton. *African American Healers*. (New York: John Wiley & Sons, Inc., 2000), p. 63-69.

Hayden, Robert C. *II African American Doctors*. (Frederick, MD.: Twenty-First Century Books, 1992), p. 186-203.

Morais, Herbert M. *The History of the Negro in Medicine*. (New York: Publishers, Inc., 1967), p. 74-75.

Sammons, Vivian Ovelton. *Blacks in Science and Medicine*. (New York: Hemisphere Publishing Corporation, 1990), p. 251.

Yount, Lisa. *Black Scientists*. (New York: Facts On File, Inc., 1991), p. 1-13.

PART TWO

LATER INNOVATORS

Dr. William Montague Cobb

Born in Washington, D.C. (1904-1990)

MD Howard Medical School 1929; PhD Case Western Reserve 1932.

Physician-Anatomist-Anthropologist-Teacher-Crusader-Writer

William, the child, was eager
    to learn about animal life;
    an eagerness sparked by a book,
    his great great grandmother's.
This eighteen seventy-one book
    influenced the career path he took.

Visiting animals in the D.C. zoo
    was a long walk for him and friends.
Walking prepared him for the future
    as a winning long distance runner.
He was an outstanding athlete.
    He was Dunbar High's "winning feet".

Also, he was an academic achiever;
    unfortunately, when he was double
    promoted became the smallest, smart
    boy in the sixth grade class!
William lost some battles that year.
    By grade seven he had no fear.

Graduation from Dunbar High;

    scholarship to Amherst College;

    winning in track and boxing titles;

    was versatile Cobb at his best!

Excelling in more than one category-

    the essence of William's life story.

He studied embryology to

    learn how living things grow.

He developed his laboratory skills

    and knowledge about biology

Studying medicine at Howard U. in D.C.

    the senior year he was a teaching appointee.

After finishing the internship

    he delayed private practice plans

    to study with Dr. Thomas W. Todd;

    thereby changing his view of anatomy.

He now thought it the core of physical life;

    the study of life, its forms and strife.

As an assistant professor of anatomy

    he became a popular lecturer.

5,500 students over the years,

    endorse him as the greatest.

When he lectured the students came
    eagerly, supporting his "full house" fame.

Dr. Cobb's achievement and involvement
    in medicine and the community are
    legendary; as was his role as a writer
    about Blacks' contribution to medicine.
His monographs and biographies exceed
    over seven hundred left for us to read.

Dr. Cobb received many diverse
    awards and honorary degrees
    that attest to his passion for
    knowledge, truth, equality, justice,
    civil rights, and the right to good health.
His former students are our nation's wealth.

Sources

Hayden, Robert C. *II African American Doctors*. (Frederick, MD.: Twenty-first Century Books, 1992), p. 72-87.

Matney, William. *Who's Who Among Black Americans*. (Lake Forest, Illinois: Educational Communications, Inc., 1985), p. 166.

Morais, Herbert, M. *The History of the Negro in Medicine*. (New York: Publishers Company, Inc., 1967), p. 142-144; 151, 159, 175, 182, 194.

Sammons, Vivian Ovelton. *Blacks in Science and Medicine*. (New York: Hemisphere Publishing Corporation, 1990), p. 57.

Dr. Daniel A. Collins

Born Darlington, South Carolina 1914
DDS Meharry Medical College 1941;
MS Denistry University of California 1944
Dentist, Research Scientist, Health Educator, Oral Pathologist,
Writer

In high school Dan's self-esteem
    was not always very high.
Teasing about his weight didn't seem
    to undermine his learning success.

His math teacher encouraged him
    to increase his study efforts
    or chances for a career were slim.
Dan listened and applied himself.

His success in all subjects
    was greatly improved.
He entered college with prospects
    -being a construction engineer.

After graduation his first career
    choice was the family business.
Certain conditions made it clear

this was not a good choice.

Dan decided to become a physician.
    He applied to two universities
    but not one had an open position,
    except dentistry at Meharry.

So it was the latter's gain
    it became a new career path.
In nineteen forty-one his name –
    became Doctor Daniel Collins.

New York City was the next phase;
    Guggenheim Dental Clinic;
California, a new trail to blaze;
    important findings in dentistry.

His California research career
    in Vitamin D and its effects –
too much not good it was clear;
    especially true for children.

Another research area was pain.
    While studying causes and cures
He was able to explain
    The phantom pain of amputees.

Dr. Collins faced some issues
    that changed his direction, but
    research with animal tissues
    was the unexpected open door.

He wrote about family health care
    He was interested in diversity
He wanted representation fair
    in books about minority achievers.

Sources

Hayden, Robert C. *II African American Doctors*. (Frederick MD: Twenty-First Century Books. 1992), p. 102-123.

PBS KQED, 1999.

http://www/pbs.org/kqed/fillmore/learning/peo

Sammons, Vivian Ovelton. *Blacks in Science and Medicine*. (New York: Hemisphere Publishing Corporation, 1990), p. 59.

Who's Who Among Black Americans. (Northbrook, IL: Who's Who Among Black Americans Publishing Co., 1985), p. 173.

Dr. Angella D. Ferguson

Born in Washington, D.C. (1925)
Overseer Howard U. Hospital Construction
Pediatrics, Sickle Cell Research, Teaching

By her high school junior year
 Angella D. Ferguson knew
 her career path was clear –
 secretary and then business.
Thanks to Angella's father
 another choice was college.
She found that she would rather
 study science and maybe medicine.

Then on to medicine and Howard U.
 She was where she wanted to be.
Graduation- then internship to do.
 It was working with children.
They became her medical mission.
 It was pediatrics, helping children.
When she became a private physician
 She found some questions unanswered.

She left private practice to find
 some of the answers through research.

Her research findings were color blind-

    they were new ideas for all children.

With great energy and concern

    she worked with sickle cell patients.

There was still much to learn

    about symptoms and treatment.

Again, there was a professional call.

    Howard University Hospital

    needed someone to "carry the ball"

    to oversee its new construction.

With logic, devotion, and vision

    Dr. Ferguson guided the work.

There were battles for each decision;

    then the world class hospital was done!

Now another battle to fight.

    The neighborhood children thought

    it great fun to knock out a light.

Parking lot lights were quite costly.

    What to do for lights and land?

Dr. Ferguson had a clever plan.

    She extended a welcome hand-

    a children's tour of the hospital.

They embraced the hospital as theirs.

    There was a Thanksgiving dinner on site.

They became a "Courtesy Patrol" that cares.

    What awesome demonstrations

    of what creative people can do

    that can grow through generations

    to better neighborhood relations.

Orange courtesy jackets were everywhere;

    serving the hospital in many ways.

No broken lights; no one would dare!

    They were helping whenever asked.

Thanks to Dr. Ferguson for heeding

    Howard U. Hospital's call

    and for the fertile seeding

    of the field of health research.

Sources

Carwell, Hattie. *Blacks in Science: Astrophysicist to Zoologist.* (Hicksville, New York: Exposition Press, 1977), p. 58.

Ebony. Chicago Publishing Co. September 1963. p. 86-92.

Hayden, Robert C. *II African American Doctors*. Frederick, (Maryland: Twenty-First Century Books, 1992), p. 154-169.

Sullivan, Otha Richard. Haskins, Jim, general editor. *African American Women Scientists and Inventors*. (New York: John Wiley & Sons, Inc., 2002), p. 72-76.

Wina Marché

Dr. Charles Richard Drew

Born in Washington, D.C. (1904-1950)
M.D. McGill 1933 Research in Blood Plasma;
Organization of National Blood Banks;
Professor of Surgery-Howard U.
Chief Surgeon/Medical Director-Freedman's Hospital

Charles Drew was an athletic star
    whose skill took him far.
A football scholarship for college;
    one step forward to higher knowledge.

Next came medical school-McGill
    the door to dreams he hoped to fulfill;
    graduation and more medical advances,
    research and teaching- more chances.

Dr. Charles R. Drew
    Howard professor, knew what to do
    to train surgeons who were the best;
    who could score very high on any test.

Today when we need a blood transfusion
    it's easily done without confusion.
Blood plasma storage now means

saved lives at emergency scenes.

Dr. Charles Richard Drew –

he knew what to do

about blood storage and banks.

To his family for sharing him, thanks!

Sources

Cox, Clinton. *African American Healers.* (New York: John Wiley & Sons, Inc., 2000), p. 100-108.

Hayden, Robert C. *II African American Doctors.* (New York: Twenty-First Century Books, 1992), 170-185.

Sammons, Vivian Ovelton. *Blacks in Science and Medicine.* (New York: Hemisphere Publishing Corporation, 1990), p. 78.

Yount, Lisa. *Black Scientists.* (New York: Facts on File, 1991), p. 54-65.

Wina Marché

Dr. Lloyd Albert Quarterman

(1918-1982) Philadelphia, Pennsylvania
Nuclear Physicist; Nuclear Chemist; Honorary Doctor of Science
Worked on the Atomic Bomb (Manhattan Project)

St. Augustine College
   and Northwestern U.
      helped to shape
         Quarterman's view
          of physics,
            chemistry and
              things universal;
                such as life being
                  a continual
                    rehearsal.

He didn't know
   he'd be a factor
      in a team
         developing a
           nuclear reactor.

Sources

Brodie, James Michael. *Created Equal: The Lives and Ideas of Black American Innovators.* (New York: William Morrow and Company, Inc., 1993), p. 165.

Ebony. Chicago: Johnson Publishing Co. September, 1949. p. 28.

"100 Years of African American Excellence in Science". *Ebony.* Chicago: Johnson Publishing Co. December, 1999. p. 84-86.

Van Sertima, Ivan, editor. *Blacks in Science: Ancient and Modern.* (New Brunswick: Transaction Books, 1992), p. 266-272.

Dr. Lawnie Taylor

1902 – Physicist; PhD University of Southern California
Solar Technologist NASA

Most of the things we grow and eat
    need the aid of solar heat.
The sun is the center of most things,
    for some happiness and sunlight it brings.
We on earth orbit around the sun.
    It never goes out or on the run.
Lawnie Taylor, a solar technologist,
    knew how the sun and things coexist.

NASA and Columbia U.
    have shared Taylor's research too;
as have Xerox Corporation
    and other entities in our nation.
Taylor's main research evolved
    around problems solar energy solved.
He volunteered much time
    to projects he considered prime.

Sources

Black Contributors to Science and Energy Technology. U.S. Government Pamphlet of 24 Biographical Sketches of Black Inventors Who Made Contributions in the Field of Energy. p. 25.

http://www.math.buffalo.edu/mad/physics/taylor_lawnie.html
http://www.em.doc.gov/hc/friend.html
http://www.em.doe.gov/laswelcome.html

Dr. Jane Cooke Wright

Born in New York City (1919); MD New York Medical College - 1925
Physician; Surgeon; Cancer Research in Chemotherapy;
Professor of Surgery; Daughter of Dr. Louis T. Wright

For Jane Cooke Wright
The future looked very bright.
Her chosen career was in art,
Then Jane had a change of heart.

Dr. Dad's views did overrule.
So, Jane chose medical school.
However, he did mention the fact
That medical school was no easy act.

No matter, Jane's mind was now clear
She wanted to join her Dad's career;
Researching a cure for cancer;
Joining the quest for an answer.

Jane Cooke Wright, MD
Her research helped people to be cancer free
She tested cancer drug combinations
With tissue cultures and drug relations.

Dr. Wright's research contribution

And findings take us steps closer to a solution.

Research always leads to advances and progress

That may some day mean total success.

Sources

Haber, Louis. *Black Pioneers of Science and Invention*. (New York: Harcourt Brace Jovanovich, 1970), p. 211, 215.

Hayden, Robert C. *II African American Doctors*. (New York: Twenty-First Century Books, 1992), p. 124-137.

Younts, Lisa. *Black Scientists*. (New York: Facts On File, Inc., 1991), p. 67-77.

Sullivan, Otha Richard. Haskins, Jim, general editor. *African American Women Scientists and Inventors*. (New York: John Wiley & Sons, Inc., 2002), p. 56-61.

Dr. Ernest J. Wilkins, Jr.

b. 1923 Chicago
PhD Age 19 University of Chicago
Worked on the Atomic Bomb (Manhattan Project)
Physicist-Mathematician-Mechanical Engineer-Nuclear Engineer

The son of an Assistant
    Secretary of Labor, Wilkins, Jr.
was brilliant, persistent,
    and a multi-faceted scientist.

Actually, Wilkins, Jr. had four
    titles physicist, mechanical engineer,
nuclear engineer and more,
    mathematician too.

Wilkins, Jr. was with a project
    connected with the atomic bomb.
Obviously of very high intellect,
    His work was often high profile.

When he was almost seventeen
    he received his first college degree.
By age nineteen the college scene
    offered another degree, a PhD

Sources

Brodie, James Michael. *Created Equal; The Lives of Black American Innovators*. (New York: William Morrow and Company, Inc., 1993), p. 165.

Carwell, Hattie. *Blacks in Science: Astrophysicist to Zoologist*. (Hicksville, New York: Exposition Press, 1977), p. 44-45.

Low, Augustus, and Clift, Virgil A. editors. *Encyclopedia of Black America*. (New York: McGraw Hill, 1984), p. 941.

McKissack, Patricia and McKissack, Frederick. *African American Scientists*. (Brookfield, Connecticut: Milbrook Press, 1994), p. 86.

PART THREE

MODERN INNOVATORS

Dr. Dale Brown Emeagwali

Baltimore, Maryland
Scientist; Microbiologist Georgetown University School of Medicine;
PhD, 1981
National Technical Association's (NTA) Scientist of the Year" Award

Dr. Dale Brown Emeagwali,
    portrait of an achiever;
    an example of a believer
    in a liberal education
    for a "knowing" nation.

Dr. Dale Brown Emeagwali;
    role model, inspirator;
    advocate, youth motivator;
    NTA awardee
    in microbiology and biochemistry.

Dr. Dale Brown Emeagwali,
    youth science volunteer;
    promoting science as a career;
    keeping expectations high;
    helping youth reach for the sky.

Dr. Dale Brown Emeagwali,
    role model, wife;
    mother, celebrator of life;
    intellect, poet, writer;
    science literacy fighter.

Dr. Dale Brown Emeagwali,
    researcher, with biological finds,
    professor, shaper of minds;
    guiding new vision, diversity
    for student growth at the university.

Sources

Givens, Willie. "Baltimorean Dale Emeagwali honored as Scientist of the Year" *Afro-American* November, 1996. Baltimore, Maryland. p. 1-5.

Henderson, Ashyia N., editor. *Contemporary Black Biography (Detroit: Gale Group. V. 31, 2002), p. 65-67.*

Henderson, Ashyia N., editor. *Who's Who Among African Americans.* (Detroit: Gale Group- Thomson Learning, 2001), p. 391.

http:www.emeagwali.com/dale/afro_american_1996.html

Matney, William C. *Who's Who Among Black Americans.* (Lake Forest, Illinois: Educational Communications, Inc., 1985), p.445.

Dr. Mary Styles Harris

1949 - Nashville, Tennessee

Biologist-Geneticist

Lincoln U.; PhD-Cornell U. 1975; Post Doctoral- Rutgers, 1976-77

The brilliance, skill, and knowledge
    Dr. Harris shares with the nation
was nurtured by school and college.
    Lincoln's, Cornell's and Rugers' education
prepared her for leadership roles;
    producing for public television;
helping medical students reach goals;
    the sickle cell directorship decision.

Dr. Harris' diverse skill and ability
    have earned her numerous commendations.
As a National Science Foundation grantee
    she wrote, produced, gave narration
for Georgia t.v. science shows.
    Her work as biologist and geneticist
placed her on boards, in t.v. studios,
    in classrooms, or wherever called to assist.

Wina Marché

Sources

Brown, Mitchell E. The Faces of Science: African Americans in The
Sciences.
http://www.Princeton.edu/~mcbrown/display/mary_harris.html. 2-
19-2001.

Ebony. Nov. 1981. p. 108, 110.

Jet. "Doctor Gets Grant to Simplify Medicine on T.V. February 21,
1980. p. 27.

Sammons, Vivian O. *Blacks in Science and Medicine.* (New York:
Hemisphere Publishers, 1990) p. 112-113.

Dr. Shirley Ann Jackson

1946 Washington, D.C.
PhD Massachusetts Institute of Technology, 1970
Physicist; President of Rensselaer Polytechnic Institute

Dr. Jackson is from MIT
    where she taught after her PhD
She was also a pioneer
    as tenured professor and peer
in the Physics Department.
    Much research time was spent
sharing her knowledge across the continent
    and gathering honors wherever she went.

Dr. Jackson's area of expertise
    took her many places overseas;
like Geneva, Sicily to work on projects
    with other nuclear physics intellects;
to Ecole d'Ete de Physique Theorique- France;
    chair of the USNRC;* an advance;
chair of INCRA** another entrance
    into the gender race "first" circumstance.

*USNRC – U.S. Nuclear Regulatory Commission
**INCRA – International Nuclear Regulatory Commission

Sources

Ebony. Chicago: Johnson Publishing Co. December 1999. p. 90

Ebony. Chicago: Johnson Publishing Co. July 1986, p. 134.

McKissack, Patricia and McKissack, Frederick. *African American Scientists*. (Brookfield, Connecticut: Milbrook Press. 1994), p. 66-90.

Sullivan, Otha Richard. Haskins, Jim, general editor. *African American Women Scientists & Inventors*. (New York: John Wiley & Sons, Inc., 2002), p. 97-99.

Dr. Roland Owens

(1960) Baltimore, Maryland Senior Investigator
Molecular Biologist: Research in Diabetes
Discovered a Virus to be Used in Gene Therapy
NIH: NIH Black Scientists' Association

Dr. Owens and colleagues felt
    the sting when the race card was dealt
at school, at work, at play.
    So, they wanted others who fell prey
to understand the game and win
    and to know the moves, the discipline.
They pondered how best to do this.
    They needed to trump, not hit and miss.

Here's the idea that came to them;
    very impressive; its an acronym,
NIHBSA.
    Here's what those last three letters say –
Black Scientists' Association-
    for recruitment – indoctrination.
Dr. Owens and the association
    want more of them in the NIH organization.

His family certainly knew

    Owens needed a brighter, larger view

than the city streets of Baltimore

    They knew life had much more in store-

like the joy, pride, and intrigue

    of being a scientist in the published league.

Let's salute Owens and the NIHBSA sisters and brothers

    for caring, mentoring, and recruiting others.

Sources

http://www.niddk.nih.gov/intram/peple/rowens.htm

http://www.hihgov/news/HIH-Record/08_27_96/story04.htm

http://63.107.122.9:913/mentors/rowens.HTM

Schulte, Brigid. "One doctor tries to change the establishment from the inside". *Detroit Free Press* Washington Bureau. August 4, 1998. p. 9F.

Dr. Bertram O. Fraser-Reid

b. 1934-Jamaica
PhD Duke U. Durham, N.C.
College Professor-
Award Winning Research Scientist-Carbohydrates

For Bertram's Jamacian kin,
    the year nineteen thirty-four
brought happiness – a baby boy!
    But happiness had a twin-
Sadness, also, came through their door.
    Death claimed their mother, their joy!
Thus began Bertram's sojourn here;
    motherless within his first year!

Father, like Mother, was educated;
    they both had teaching careers.
Bertram, too, felt the "call to teach".
    Later he chose a field unrelated
at the end of five teaching years.
    Chemistry seemed within his reach.
Bertram then became self-taught
    using a chemistry book he bought.

From Canada came his first degree;
    Queens University, the venue.
Then it was research, assist, observe.
    Bertram saw research as a key;
to understanding things old and new;
    a chance to discover, to serve.
His interest, sugar, a carbohydrate,
    to living things how does it relate?

Two more degrees more knowledge-
    assisting winner of Nobel Prize,
Sir Derek Burton's, lab work
    London's Imperial College
talented chemists there could advise
    was any student's learning "perk".
Then back in Canada to new
    University Waterloo.

Bertram received an award
    in nineteen seventy-five
for a new sugar finding.
    It turned researchers' toward
a substitute petroleum drive
    for "petro" needs less binding.
Industries that were "petroleum lead"
    could now use sugar instead.

Next, he comes to the United States;

    soon he and his colleagues found

ways to synthesize with ease.

    They discovered sugar traits

That could be the very ground

    work for a curing a disease.

Chemicals that are "low cost"

    lower the number of consumers lost.

His work could have other uses

    Such as insect pest control

to stop destruction of trees.

    Bertram's research also produces

ways to study simple sugar's role

    in how the body fights disease.

His carbohydrate work tells

    how molecules relate to cells.

Sources

Driven by Sugar". *Black Enterprise*. February, 1990, p. 86.

Mabunda, Mpho L., editor. *The African American Almanac*. (Detroit: Gale Research, Inc., 1997), p. 1075.

Stucky, William K. "A Strong and Unusual Nobel Contender". *Leader*. September 14, 1989.

Yount, Lisa. *Black Scientists American Profile:* (New York: Facts on File, 1991), p. 80-91.

John P. Moon

(1938) Philadelphia
Computer Engineer

John Moon's computer career
    started years ago
    as a child whose actions
    had words like
    take apart, repair, rebuild.
He was a budding engineer.

His quest for knowledge
    continued; a Bachelor of Science
    Mechanical Engineering
    Masters degree.
    He mastered
    the ritual of college

Moon entered the computer field
    a Black recruit,
    IBM,
    self-taught
    in computers.
Self-teaching had a positive yield.

Finding solutions his task.

    with IBM teams

    of engineers,

    of physicists

    of chemists.

He'd find answers to questions they'd ask.

He joined other computer companies;

    Micronetics,

    Tandem Magnetics,

    Apple Computers,

    in new cities.

Moon contributed and advanced with ease.

His world of computer technology

    is now everyday stuff

    with new words such as

    disk drives, floppy disks,

    software, hardware.

Moon is now an Apple Computer V.P.

Sources

Black Enterprise. "Master of the Hard Drive". February, 1990, p. 80.

Sullivan, Otha Richard. Haskins, Jim, general editor. *African American Inventors*. (New York: John Wiley & Sons, 1998), p. 132-136.

Yount, Lisa. *Black Scientists*. (New York: Facts on File, 1991). p. 94-104.

PART FOUR

INSPIRATORS

Inspirers and Inspirators*

Sometimes the English dictionary

has meanings that are contrary

to what one wishes to say

    or the word doesn't have the sway

        or the right vim or vigor

            or it needs to be smaller or bigger.

"Inspire" is a word like that.

    That it means to motivate is a fact;

        add an "r" does it ring like "innovator"

            where the move from "innovate" is greater?

            Now listen to the word "inspirer"

                The "er" doesn't give it much fire!

So here is a non-dictionary word,

    "inspirator", one you have never heard.

        "Inventor" is most respectable and fine

          "innovator" is great and has spine,

            if words have spine. Without hesitation

                wouldn't you say "inspirator" goes with

                "inspiration?"

So if you agree to this derivation

"inspirer" has a new designation.

So, this book is about invention,

that is still our intention,

innovation and inspiration

and those in our nation

who shall be called

inventors,

innovators,

and

inspirators*.

The word inspirator* *Copyright by Wina Marché 2003-pending.*

Parents as Inspirators

Parents are their children's
    initial inspirator.
They are the ultimate
    positive motivator.
Parent does not always
    mean "by birth".
Relatives, friends can
    booster self-worth.
You know what folk mean
    about self-worth and self-esteem
if you truly believe
    you are okay.
You'll be fine and whatever
    you do success will come your way.

The Detroit parents of the
    eight Green girls,
Rev. and Mrs. Havious Green,
    showed them the best of worlds.
Their world included a positive
    and structured atmosphere
with each girl believing she
    could succeed in any career.

And succeed they did; every one
    is either an MD or PhD
The parents, the inspirators, helped
    the eight daughters see
it is possible to achieve;
    to be whatever they wished to be.

There are many African American
    families whose story of success
has motivated many readers
    through national or local press.
Another such family is the
    Thorntons, Father and Mother,
Donald and Tass plus siblings
    six and not one brother.
Donald formed his girls into
    a traveling musical band

That performed throughout the
    country, mostly college land.
Money earned was used to help
    the girls attend college.
If they were to be doctors
    they needed knowledge.
The struggle was hard, Father
    was a ditch digger.

Was his dream for his

    daughters really bigger

than a ditch digger

    was supposed to dream?

As a family they worked

    hard as an entertaining team.

Thornton was the planner

    and the master inspirator.

Poverty was not in his plan

    their lives would be greater.

Though he did not get

    six Thornton MD's,

he was happy with their degrees.

All of the ditch digger's girls

    had professional positions,

        science department head,

        court stenographer,

        dentist,

          nurse,

            two physicians.

Sources

Culp, Deborah. "A 21st Century Family – the Greens." *The NAACP Reporter*, Winter, 1992, p. 4. Detroit, Michigan.

Thornton, Yvonne S., M.D., *The Ditchdigger's Daughters: A Black Family's Astonishing Success Story*. (New York: Penguin Books, 1996).

Teachers as Inspirators*

Perhaps, you had a teacher who

made you pause a moment to

think about something said

or about a book you read.

Maybe teacher shared an idea

that made you think about a career.

Maybe you had some self-doubt

hidden by a frown and a pout.

Teacher could see through the facades;

helped you achieve against the odds.

Many moons and many years later

you'll remember and thank this

inspirator*!

Wina Marché

Milla Granson

Kentucky and Mississippi (b. in 1800s)
Risked Her Life to Teach Others
An Inspirator*

Milla Granson, a slave girl,
    tried to expand her small world
    by learning to read and write
    and helping others ease their plight.

Milla taught other slaves at night
    as they came in danger and in fright;
    though it was illegal for them to read,
    they wanted their minds to be freed.

Secretly each night at twelve o'clock,
    quietly, determined, without a knock,
    they came through Milla's cabin door
    and joined the shadows on the floor.

Milla taught them all she knew.
    They learned to read and write, too.
    Using their new and secret skills
    they escaped to distant valleys and hills.

After taking the forbidden classes,

    they wrote their own freedom passes;

    despite the risk, they took the dare

    for a chance to breathe sweet freedom's air!

Milla's gift to her generation

    was a teacher's ultimate declaration

    of how a quest can be sustained

    by the spirit seeking to be unchained!

Sources

Dannett, Sylvia G. L. *Profiles of Negro Womanhood 1600-1900*. (Yonkers, New York: Educational Heritage, 1964), p. 74.

Grim, Valerie. Hine, Darlene Clark, ed. *Black Women in America: An Historical Encyclopedia*. (Brooklyn, New York: Carlson Publishing, Inc., 1993), p. 498.

http://www.awomanaweek.comGranson.html

http://www.ccsu.edu/WomenCtr/newsletter_pages

PART FIVE

EARLY INSPIRATORS IN MEDICINE

Early African American Medics

Bondage brought them,
    with their
    knowledge,
    and skill;
    determination,
    that saved lives,
    eased pain,
    despite their own.

They came
    unwillingly,
    with exotic
    names,
    Cesar,
    Papan,
    Primus,
    Onesimus,
    and touched
    many lives.

James Derham (Durham)
    was among them.
    born in bondage,
    sold,

    bought,
    and moved
through the lives of
Dr. John Kearsley;
Dr. George West;
Dr. Robert Dove.

Dr. Dove,
in appreciation,
made Derham
a free man.
By 1788,
at age 26,
James Derham
was a highly
skilled New
Orleans doctor.

Though in
    bondage
    Cesar,
    Papan,
    Primus,
    Derham
    brought
    knowledge,

skill and,

human

kindness

that healed

and saved

lives.

Sources

Cox, Clinton and Haskins, Jim, General Editor. *African American Healers*. (New York: John Wiley & Sons, Inc., 2000), p. 1, 6-9.

Hayden, Robert C. *II African American Doctors*. (New York: Twenty-First Century Books, 1992), p. 9-17.

Sammons, Vivian Ovelton. *Blacks in Science and Medicine*. (New York: Hemisphere Publishing Corporation, 1990), p. 52, 73, 182, 184, 195.

Morais, Herbert Montfort. *The History of the Negro In Medicine* (New York: Publishers Co., 1967), p. 5-7, 8-10.

Wina Marché

Dr. Lucas Santomee

First Black U.S. Doctor
New York 1600s

The first Black doctor in the U.S.
    was Dr. Lucas Santomee.
In Holland he studied with success
    earning a medical degree.
In New York he gave medical care
    and acquired certain lands
    given by the officials there
in gratitude for his medical hands.

Sources

http://www.freedomtrail.org/timelineall.asp
http://www.blackfirsts.com/blacksfirst_name.a
Saunders, Doris E., editor. *The Ebony Handbook by Editors of Ebony.*
    (Chicago: Johnson Publishing Co., 1974), p. 362.
Sammons, Vivian Ovelton. *Blacks in Science and Medicine.* (New
    York: Hemisphere Publishing Corporation, 1990), p. 209.

Martin Robison Delaney

Born in Charlestown, West Virginia (1812-1885)
Physician; Spokeman against Fugitive Slave Law;
Leader in Chlorea Fight 1854

Delaney chose medicine
    at age nineteen.
He studied medicine
    as an apprentice with
    three different doctors.

Delaney went to Harvard's
    Medical School for a
    short time and left to join
    the fight for freedom against
    the fugitive slave law.

There was great danger in
    traveling even for a free Black;
    he was beaten up in Ohio.
    He continued speaking out
    at home and in other countries.

Delaney returned to the
    practice of medicine in

Pittsburgh. He was a leader
in the fight against the
1854 chlorea epidemic.

Sources

Cox, Clinton. Haskins, Jim, general editor, *African American Healers*.
(New York: John Wiley & Sons, Inc., 2000), p. 17-22.

Logan, Rayford W., Winston, Michael R., editors. *Dictionary of American Negro Biography*. (1st edition. New York: Norton, 1983), p. 169-172.

Morais, Herbert Montfort. *The History of the Negro in Medicine*.
(New York: Publishers Co., 1967), p. 27-29, 35.

White, Deborah, Gray. *Let My People Go: African Americans 1804-1860*. (New York: Oxford University Press, 1996), p. 113-114, 120, 122, 132.

Dr. James McCune Smith

(1811-1865) Physician; University of Glasgow 1837
Born Free in New York

Dr. James McCune Smith,
>   was born free.
>   In a another country
>   earned his medical degree.

Scotland was the country,
>   University of Glasgow
>   did the history making
>   honor in 1837.

He helped make life
>   better in New York
>   as physician, as a citizen,
>   as a pharmacy operator.

He was a great
speaker, writer
and defender of the
right of Blacks to be doctors.

Sources

Cox, Clinton, Haskins, Jim, general editor. *African American Healers*. (New York: John Willey & Sons, Inc., 2000), p. 10-14.

Kaufman, Martin, Gallishoff, Stuart, and Savitt, Todd L., editors. *Dictionary of American Medical Biography*. (Westport, CT: Greenwood Press, 2 vols. 1984), p. 693.

Sammons, Vivian Ovelton. *Blacks in Science and Medicine*. (New Hemisphere: Publishing Corporation, 1990), p. 215-216.

White, Deborah Gray. *Let My People Go: African Americans 1804-1860*. (New York: Oxford University Press, 1996), p. 106.

Dr. Nathan Francis Mossell

Hamilton, Ontario Canada (1856-1946)
Physician; Activist, Writer
First Black Graduate Medical School of the University of
Pennsylvania, 1882

Dr. Mossell's parents chose
    to live in the U.S.
His parents thought
    the move was the best
they could do to find
    a good school
where segregated classes
    was not the rule.

The family returned to
    the United States
hoping the Civil War's end
    and public mandates
would find the mood
    for integration
good and embraced by
    most in the nation.

Wina Marché

Father lead the fight
    to integrate
the school of Lockport
    in New York State.
Son, Nathan Mossell finished
    high school and college.
He began his pursuit
    of medical knowledge.

The University of Pennsylvania
    was his first choice.
He had some cause
    to rejoice.
He was accepted but
    that was only part
of a battle that took
    grit and much heart.

The first day in class he was
    asked to sit behind a screen.
He of course refused; he had been
    accepted by the dean!
He sat on a bench; no
    one would sit near.
Not his problem; it was theirs
    it was clear.

On graduation day applause
 for him was long and loud.
He had conquered the attitudes
 now one and all were proud.
The provost had to ask
 the crowd to stop.
Dr. Mossell graduated fourth,
 in his class, from the top!

Let's commend his strength
 in those tough days.
We know Dr. Mossell
 received accolades
for the medical facility
 he found
to help students who were
 medical career bound.

Sources

Cox, Clinton and Haskins, Jim, general editor. *African American Healers* (New York: John Wiley and Sons, 2000), p. 58-62.

Logan, Rayford W., Winston, Michael R. Editors. *Dictionary of American Negro Biography*. 1st edition. (New York: Norton, 1983), p. 457-458.

McKissack, Patricia, and McKissack, Frederick. *African American Scientists*. (Brookfield, Connecticut: The Millbrook Press, 1994), p. 43.

Morais, Herbert Monfort. *The History of Negroes in Medicine*. (New York: Publishers Co., 1967), p. 79-82.

Dr. William A. Hinton

Born in Chicago; 1883-1959;

MD Harvard Medical College with Honors 1912

Physician, Bacteriologist, Pathologist;

Harvard Medical School Professor

Designer of the Hinton Test;

William A Hinton's life
Is an inspiration in how
To follow a dream despite strife
Not give up and bow
To defeat when things don't workout;
And not to give in to self-doubt.

His parents were not born free,
They wanted William to have a chance
To be whatever he wished to be;
Have a choice whatever the circumstance.
They wanted his education to be the best
To assure his readiness whatever the test.

To be a surgeon was his dream.
Hinton finished high school at sixteen
Then spent two years in academe.
His money was short and lean.

And one door closed after two years,
But he had a plan to allay all fears.

Then at Harvard there came an open door.
Medical School was the existing plan.
But money was an issue once more.
Four years of college teaching began.
Medicine was still in his mind and heart
As Harvard's Medical School set to start.

Hinton was a member of that first class.
The year was 1909.
Nine years after what seemed an impasse!
His Harvard grades were just fine
For a much needed scholarship twice.
Work and study meant constant sacrifice.

His knowledge of disease detection
Opened yet another medical door
For teaching a medical lab section.
He had taken the time to study and explore
While working to save for medical school.
He finished in three years; four was the rule!

1912 was the year!
It was time for his medical internship.

Closed hospital doors did interfere!

This step he was forced to skip!

The politics of ancient days

Made him learn this phase other ways

He worked mornings as a volunteer

In pathology in a hospital run by the state.

The route he took was rough but clear.

He couldn't let politics negate

His ambition, determination, and fire.

Practicing medicine was his desire.

On his evening job he was paid.

No patients just their blood sample.

It became a learning crusade.

The knowledge he gained was ample

Enough to invent a new blood test.

The Hinton Test – history tells the rest!

Hinton didn't fulfill his dreams,

But the field of medicine was blessed.

His dream was not meant to be it seems.

His research, writing and Hinton Test

Were important to human health.

They were his talent, his destiny, his wealth!

Hinton's impact on medicine was great.

He struggled long against many blocks

The direction life took him was not straight

But filled with closed doors, some without locks!

At each closed door or political no,

He paused, regrouped, continued to grow!

Sources

Cobb, W. Montague. William Augustus Hinton, M.D., 1883-. National Medical Association, *Journal*, v. 49, Nov. 1957, 427-428.

Cox, Clinton. Haskins, Jim, general editor. *African American Healers*. (New York: John Wiley & Sons, Inc., 2000), p. 94-99.

Franklin, John Hope and Moss, Jr. Alfred A. *Up from Slavery*. 7th edition. (New York: McGraw-Hill, Inc., 1994), p. 410, 414.

Hayden, Robert. *11 African American Doctors*. (Frederick, MD.: Twenty-First Century Books, 1992.), p. 36-51.

Jet, Chicago: Johnson Publishing Co., August 27, 1959, p. 12.

Sammons, Vivian Ovelton. *Blacks in Science and Medicine*. (New York: Hemisphere Publishing Corporation, 1990), p. 121-122.

PART SIX

MODERN INSPIRATORS IN MEDICINE

Dr. Keith Black

b. 1958 Auburn, Alabama
University of Michigan Medical School – 1981 Neurosurgeon
Director Cedars-Sinai Maxine Dunitz
Neurosurgical Institute, Los Angeles
Discoverer of Bradykinin;

Young, Black, and gifted – his name?
    Dr. Keith Black- his claim to fame?
Besides being young, gifted, and Black
    he's on the "determined to cure cancer track".
Noted for success as a surgeon for brain
    cancer. He has global respect and acclaim.
Brain cancer patients come from everywhere
    to place themselves in Dr. Black's care.

In the over two hundred operations a year
    many of the patients' cases are severe.
He is considered the world's best.
    Some think his surgical hands are blest.
Still others think his "no touch operation"
    theory and his professed adulation
of the "sacredness" of the brain
    are factors in the success he does attain.

Because the brain is easy to agitate

    Dr. Black prefers to "sneak in" to operate.

The brain moves like jello to the touch,

    making it easy to remove too much.

Another problem- chemotherapy;

    it is most often than not a calamity.

It kills the healthy and the cancerous tissue.

    Not removing enough is another issue.

An avid researcher, Black has found three

    approaches to brain surgery that might agree

with the patient or at least decrease adverse

    conditions that leave the patient feeling worse.

One is his discovery of bradykinin,

    a bodily substance that allows medicine

to reach only the cancerous cells

    that are ready when the target area swells.

Second, getting the patient's own body to enter the fight

    with its immune system and attack cancer might

be a solution. Third, there is MedArray,

    a new science technology that's on the way.

MedArray maps out the cancer tissue, to attack,

    no harm to good brain cells; no medical drawback.

Dr. Black believes collaboration –

    scientists/physicians, equals cancer eradication.

Finally, what manner of man is he?

Skilled, dedicated, intelligent, all agree.

His parents say love of science was always there.

He says this love comes from he knows not where.

Urologist, surgeon, wife, Carolyn understands

it all comes from his skilled surgical hands.

Dr. Keith Black is a medical innovator;

He is for certain a modern day inspirator.

Sources

Experimental Energy. Michigan Chronicle. Detroit. February 16-22, 2001, p. 2C

Lemonick Michael. Reported by Mann, Arnold. *The Tumor War*. Time Special Issue. Fall, 1997. p. 46-52.

http://www.breakthroughtv.com/black,htm

http://www.ninds,nih.gov/biography/council_bi

Whitaker, Charles. *All Star Surgeon*. Ebony: Chicago. May, 1999, p. 146-148 +.

Wina Marché

Benjamin S. Carson, M.D.

Born 1951 Detroit, Michigan; Yale University;
University of Michigan, MD
Director, Pediatric Neurosurgery; Assistant Professor, Neurosurgery,
Oncologoy, and Pediatrics, John Hopkins University School of
Medicine; Primary Surgeon of the Pediatric Neurosurgeon Team that
Separated German Siamese Twins in 1987)

You can be
  what you wish to be.
The life of Ben Carson, MD
  shows us this
  is true.
Life depends on
  what you do.

Detroit, Michigan,
Nineteen hundred fifty-one,
Life begins for Ben Carson.
By the time he reaches age eight
He starts to question his fate.
His parents' marriage ends.
Life began downward trends.
He and brother went to Boston, Mass.
Their sojourn there didn't last.

Back in Detroit after two years

They faced the future without fears.

Mother and sons together were three.

They had dreams and plans to foresee.

School the key to their dream,

For Ben was no model academe.

They had done well in Boston, Mass.,

But Ben did poorly in his Detroit class.

When his classmates called him "dumb"

His pain was deep, quiet, and numb.

Mother's hope was in the school,

So she set down a strict rule.

More reading and less t.v.

Was his mother's stern decree.

Three t.v. programs a week.

Two books per week – things looked bleak!

Ben and brother reluctantly complied

Then their grades took an upward glide!

The library became a familiar place;

And Ben's classmates did an "about face".

He was answering questions they'd ask.

Reading became an enjoyable task!

His own goals he began to surpass.

Ben wanted to be the best in his class.

Mother told them that they were smart.

This gave Ben's self-esteem a jump start!

Ben's fervent drive and knowledge quest

Made him want to be a quiz show guest.

But Ben had two demons to suppress

Before he could really focus on success.

Peer pressure from the "in" crowd

Could put Ben Carson in a shroud!

His personal peace seemed to decrease

As peer pressure seemed to increase.

Terrible temper was out of control.

He was at risk of losing his soul.

Ben conquered "demon terrible temper" – (dtt).

And overcame "demon peer pressure" – (dpp).

Divine intervention and some anguish

He attained his "demon free" wish.

His teen and adult life reached new heights

Neurosurgery, Pediatrics new insights,

Yale, U of M, and much more –

Australia, Baltimore, and still more!

To learn more about Ben's interesting life,

With his mother, brother, children, and wife,

Read his first book, *Gifted Hands*.

His gifted hands are known in many lands!

Ben's other book, *Think Big*, gives advice

That is tried, tested, and concise.

Its purpose – to help young people achieve.

Its simple truths are easy to conceive.

Paraphrased here:

Set your goal.

Pay the toll.

Develop you gift.

Give others a lift.

Do your best.

Be prepared whatever the test.

Your Supreme Being will do the rest.

Sources

Carson, M.D., Ben, with Cecil Murphey. *Gifted Hands*. (Grand Rapids, Michigan: Zondervan Publishing House, 1990).

Carson, M.D., Ben, with Cecil Murphey. *Think Big. – Unleashing Your Potential for Excellence*. (Zondervan Publishing House: Grand Rapids, Michigan, 1992).

Cox, Clinton. *African American Healers*. (New York: John Wiley & Sons, Inc., 2000), p. 123-127.

Sammons, Vivian Ovelton. *Blacks in Science and Medicine*. New York: Hemisphere Publishing Corporation, 1990), p. 49.

Wina Marché

Dr. Arthur C. Logan

Born in Tuskegee, Alabama (1909-1973)
MD. Columbia University College of Physicians, 1934
Scholarship and Hospital Named for Him
Physician, Surgeon, Community Activist

This story is about a little boy
    at age nine about to start a new life.
New York is the place of the new life
    with a doctor sister and her doctor husband.

The little boy's family was not only
    deeply into giving medical care
    they were deeply involved in giving
    time to help solve community problems.

It was in this family life the boy grew
    and learned and formed some beliefs
about life, himself and his life calling.
    His choice of medicine was no surprise.

The boy, Arthur, entered Williams College
    in 1926 as one of six Black students.
He performed well and was graduated.
    Four years later it was medical school.

1930 was the year; Columbia
    University's College of Physicians
and Surgeons was the higher education
    institution. Graduation was 1934.

In 1936 Dr. Arthur Logan
    joined his sister and brother-in-law
in their practice of medicine
    and fight for better Harlem health care.

In 1942 Dr. Logan opened his own practice.
    From 1941-46 he did graduate study
in surgery at New York Postgraduate
    Medical School. He was a noted surgeon.

Dr. Logan was a medical leader;
    Dr. Logan was a civic leader,
    a supporter of any cause
    that helped poor Black people.

His patients (including the great
    Duke Ellington) regarded him highly.
Dr. Martin Luther King was a friend.
    A New York Hospital is named in his honor.

The Arthur C. Logan Memorial Hospital;

    his scholarship at Williams College –

    -testaments to his impact on people.

Dr. Arthur C. Logan was an inspiration.

Sources

Hayden, Robert. *II African American Doctors.* (Frederick, MD.:; Twenty-First Century Books, 1992), p. 88-101.

Mabunda, Mpho L., ed. *The African American Almanac.* (Detroit: Gale Research, 1997), p. 1075.

Sammons, Vivian Ovelton. *Blacks in Science and Medicine* (New York: Hemisphere Publishing Corporation, 1990), p. 155.

Dr. Samuel P. Massie, Jr.

Little Rock, Arkansas 1919

Iowa State University PhD - 1946

Researcher; Chemist; Professor; Patent for Antibacterial Agent

The professor has his own drum beat.

    He listens and rejects defeat.

His is the strong stand;

    no need to sound the band.

Awards, honors, speak of his success.

    Perhaps his credo is one to profess.

Confidence and endurance he instills

    in college students to develop their skills.

He taught at three universities;

    has three higher education degrees;

    was president of North Carolina College;

    noted for his chemistry knowledge.

President Lyndon Johnson named

    him professor of chemistry at famed

Annapolis Naval Academy

    a very prestigious place to be;

there more than twenty-eight years

    influencing, guiding, young naval careers.

Seventeen of those years were spent
    as chair of the chemistry department.
Throughout his career he was often a "first".
    There were times when it was the worst
    of times and then some of the time
situations had "no reason or rhyme".

Like the times at Iowa State
    isolation or rejection was his fate.
Segregation seeped throughout the dorm
    clubs, organizations. It was the norm.
Years later when receiving the college's award
    his acceptance speech was "for the record".

"From the Basement Next to the Rats"
    was the speech title-so much for facts.
His picture graces the Smithsonian wall.
    Professor Massie, one might say, "has it all".
Husband, father, scientist, mentor, molder
    of young minds, researcher, patent holder.

Dr. Massie did research for federal projects.
    The research was secret and not in context.
So, the researcher didn't know the scope
    or purpose; but for good was the hope.

He believes chemistry should help human kind

in lofty theories and in the daily grind.

Sources

American Men and Women of Science: the Physical and Biological Science. (New York: Bowker, 1971 A Continuation of 1906-1968. 16th ed.), p. 250.

http://www.doe-hbcu-massie-chair.com/

http://www.princeton.edu/~mcbrown/display/mas

Taylor, Julius, ed. *The Negro in Science* (Baltimore, Maryland: Morgan State College Press, 1955), p. 184.

Thompson, Neal. "The Chemist: An Interview with Samuel P. Massie." *American Legacy.* Spring 2001, p. 49-50; 52-53.

Wina Marché

Dr. David Satcher

(1941) Anniston, Alabama; Morehouse with Honors 1963;
Case Western Reserve – 1970 MD; PhD - 1970
U.S. Surgeon General 1998-2002

A small child's experience
    leaves a lasting impression.
It can be memories that
    bring sadness even aggression.
David had whooping cough
    things were not good.
He needed a doctor's visit
    but no White would.
The only Black doctor in
    the area came.
David's career goals were,
    from that day, never the same!

Now it was a healing
    doctor he wanted to be.
The doctor's medicine removed
    David's agony.
He thought it would
    be swell
To help children and

adults get up and get well.

David, the adult, the doctor,

    has that same belief.

He strives for individual

    and national medical relief

Dr. Satcher's career path

    touched sickle cell

Affects, treatment, and

    what these spell.

Several medical centers

    and sickle cell venues

Benefited from his medical expertise

    and administrative views.

At two medical schools,

    Morehouse and UCLA

Satcher's professorship

    was an innovative stay.

His talents include, medic, professor

    "turnabout expert".

This became known in 1982

    with a financial alert.

Meharry Medical College and

    the hospital for training

Were near accreditation loss

and financial straining.

Dr. Satcher was able to

administer a "turnabout"

Returning Meharry's original

national and international clout.

Dr. Satcher's next venue

was the CDCP

Where he sought to help

more of society

With the Center for Disease

Control Prevention.

He helped many issues receive

national medical attention.

Then came the ultimate

U. S. acclamation

He became Surgeon

General for the nation.

Satcher Chronology

Born – March 2, 1941 Anniston, Alabama

B.S. Morehosue College 1963

Case Western Reserve MD PhD 1970

1972-1975 – Director King-Drew Medical Center

1973-1975 – Associate Director King-Drew Sickle Cell Center

1973-1975 – Assistance Professor UCLA School of Medicine

1974-1976 – Professor of Chair Dept. of Family Medicine Morehouse College of Medicine

1982-1993 – President of Meharry Medical College

                Numerous Awards

1993-1998 – Director of Center for Disease Control Prevention (CDCP)

1998-2002 – United States Surgeon General

Sources

Cox, Clinton, and Haskins, Jim, general editor. *African American Healers*. (New York: John Wiley & Sons, Inc., 2000), p. 137-142.

Hess, David. "Satcher confirmed surgeon general". *Detroit Free Press*. February 11, 1998. p. 5A.

Meckler, Laura. "Surgeon general approval expected". *Detroit Free Press*. February 10, 1998.

"Satcher Directs Morehouse School of Medicine's New Center for Primary Care" *Jet*, February 4, 2002. p. 20-21.

PART SEVEN

EARLY LADY INSPIRATORS IN MEDICINE

African American Lady Medics as Inspirators

Their journey was
    difficult.
The need for
    their skill
    was great.
The early Black
    lady medics,
    were pioneers,
    were inspirators.

Their journey
    was twice as tough
    as their brother
    medics.

They like
    their brothers
    gave much
    as pioneers,
    as inspirators.

Wina Marché

Dr. Mary Edward Chinn

Great Barrington, Massachusetts (1896-1980)
Bellevue Hospital Medical College – 1926-
First Black Woman Graduate
First Black Woman Intern at Harlem Hospital;

Dr. Chinn had several
    learning transitions. She
    was a teacher- but
    a high school drop-out
    first – later she lost self-doubt.

She changed from music
    to study medicine
    a first at Harlem Hospital,
    after a degree from Bellevue;
    Dr. Chinn had other "firsts", too.

She had cause for
    self-doubt. Her father
    had his own ideas about learning;
    he rejected her educational pursuit-
    no ladies on the medical route.

No financial support from him.

Mother encouraged and helped
Chinn's quest to be a doctor.
Early cancer diagnosis and detection
was Chinn's interest and direction.

Sources

Abram, Ruth J. Sneed. *Send Us a Lady Physician: Women Doctors in .*
America, 1835-1920. (New York: Norton, 1st ed. 1986), p. 112.

Hill, Ruth Edmond, ed. *Women of Courage.* (Radcliffe, 1984), p. 14-
15.

Sammons, Vivian Ovelton, *Blacks in Science and Medicine.* (New
York: Hemisphere Publishing Corporation, 1990), p. 53.

Shifrin, Susan. Miller, Janet., Darlene Clark Hine, ed. *Black Women*
in America.; An Historical Encyclopedia (Brooklyn: Carlson
Publishing Corporation, 1993), p. 235-236.

Wina Marché

Dr. Rebecca J. Cole

(1846-1922) Philadelphia
Women's Medical College of Pennsylvania - 1867

The second U. S. Black Lady
   to receive a medical degree –
   co-founded a women's center in 1873.

She was the first graduate
   of Women's Medical College.
   Several cities shared her medical knowledge.

Sources

Abram, Ruth J., ed. *Send Us a Lady Physician; Women Doctors in America 1835-1920.* (New York: W.W. Norton, & Company, 1986), p. 113.

Galloway-Wright, Brenda. Hine, Darlene Clark, ed. *Black Women in America, an Historical Encyclopedia.* (Brooklyn: Carlson Publishing, 1993), p. 261-262.

Morais, Herbert Montfort. *The History of the Negro In Medicine.* (New York: Publishers Co., 1967), p. 317.

Ploski, Harry A. and Williams, James eds. *The Negro Almanac; A Reference Work on the Afro American.* 4th ed. (New York: Wiley, 1976), p. 1043.

Wina Marché

Dr. Rebecca Lee Crumpler

(1833) Richmond, Virginia

Female Medical College in Boston

First and Only Black to Earn Doctress of Medicine Degree- 1864

Inspirator is the word to describe

    Dr. Crumpler who in 1864

    was the first Black lady

    to open a closed medical door.

Women and children were the intended

    clients of her health care

    and book. She wanted them

    healthy, conscious, and aware.

Sources

Cox, Clinton, Haskins, Jim, general editor. *African American Healers.* (New York: John Wiley & Sons, Inc., 2000), p. 41-45.

Davis, Marianna W., editor. *Contributions of Black Women to America, Volume II.* (Columbia, South Carolina: Kenday Pres, Inc., 1981), p. 377.

Jolly, Allison. and Hine, Darlene Clark. ed. *Black Women in America, An Historical Encyclopedia.* (Brooklyn: Carlson Publishing, Inc., 1993), p. 290-291.

Morais, Herbert Montfort. *The History of the Negro in Medicine.* (New York: Publishers Co., 1967), p. 43.

Wina Marché

Dr. Matilda Arabella Evans

Aiken, South Carolina (1872-1935)
Women's Medical College of Pennsylvania, 1897
Surgeon, Educator

Dr. Evans, surgeon, was the first
    licensed lady healer
    in South Carolina.
    She was a problem solver,
    a community health care involver.

She established a hospital
    and training school;
    a public health clinic
    all services free.
    She was a youth recreation devotee.

Sources

Abram, Ruth J., ed. *Send Us a Lady Physician: Women Doctors in America 1835-1920*. (New York: Norton & Co., 1986), p. 113.

Davis, Marianna W., editor. *Contributions of Black Women to America, Volume II.* (Columbia, South Carolina; Kenday Press, Inc., 1981), p. 375.

Galloway-Wright, Brenda. Hine, Darlene Clark, ed. *Black Women in America: An Historical Encyclopedia.* (Brooklyn, New York: Carlson Publishing, Inc., 1993), p. 401-402.

Kaufman, Martin, et al, *Dictionary of American Medical Biography* (West Port, CT.: Greenwood Press, 1984), p. 234-235.

Wina Marché

Dr. Dorothy Boulding Ferebee

Norfolk, Virginia (1897-1980)
Tufts Medical School 1927 with Honors
Physician, Obstetrician

Dr. Ferebee's eight plus decade
    sojourn on earth, like
    her pioneer, sister medics,
    was an humanitarian mission
    to improve the human condition –
    as in Mississippi Health Care Aid.

The volunteer effort had the name
    MHP, as in Mississippi
    Health Project. Dr. Ferebee
    was the director. The mobile
    units with 12 doctors and staff
    treated the ill and the lame.

The year was 1935.
    Her sorority, Alpha Kappa
    Alpha sponsored the project.
    Such a volunteer effort
    was unheard of those days.
    MHP helped people survive.

She became a national leader

> in Alpha Kappa Alpha;
> National Council of Negro
> Women. Founder of the Women's
> Institute, dedicated to public
> service, a national succeeder.

She served higher education

> as a Howard U. professor
> and health service director.
> She worked with service groups
> to attain equality for Blacks;
> to eliminate discrimination.

Sources

Carwell, Hattie. *Blacks in Science: Astrophysicist to Zoologist.* (Hicksville, New York: Exposition Press, 1977), p. 58.

Ebony. May, 1964, p. 70.

Hill, Edmonds Ruth, ed. *Women of Courage: An Exhibition of Photographs.* By Judith Sedwick. (Radcliffe College, 1984), p. 9.

Jerrido, Margaret. Hine, Darlene Clark, ed. *Black Women in America: An Historical Encyclopedia.* (Brooklyn, New York: Carlson Publishing Inc., 1993), p. 425-426.

Sammons, Vivian Ovelton. *Blacks in Science and Medicine.* (New York: Hemisphere Publishing Corporation, 1990), p. 88.

Dr. Justina Laurena Ford

Knoxville, Illinois (1871-1952)

Hering Medical College, Chicago, Illinois- 1899

First African American Lady Physician in Denver, Colorado Area

A role model was Doctor Ford's life.

    Being Black and a lady

    you can guess there was strife

    from training to practice.

Colorado, the City of Denver

    was her medical base.

    Denver folk were happy to have her-

    "The Lady Doctor" on call.

Dr. Ford was truly a fighter.

    The folk at Denver Hospital

    didn't make her life brighter.

    Her patients couldn't come there!

So, "The Lady Doctor" made house calls.

    Dr. Ford served all folk-

    folk poor,-folk with sudden windfalls;

    any race, any religion, any language.

"Baby Doctor" was her other name.

> Would you believe, over seven thousand
> deliveries Dr. Ford could claim
> in over fifty years of medical practice!

Dr. Ford had time on her side

> in her struggle through the years.
> She narrowed the medical divide
> in Colorado, City of Denver.

She is truly a legend; her legacy

> her triumphs that still inspire.
> Her story, you will agree,
> is Denver, Colorado Black History.

Sources

Cox, Clinton. *African American Healers*. (New York: John Wiley & Sons, Inc., 2000), p. 81-86.

Davis, Marianna W. editor. *Contributions of Black Women to America*. Volume II (Columbia, South Carolina: Kenday Press, Inc., 1981), p. 380.

Jerrido, Margaret. Hine, Darlene Clark, ed. *Black Women in America*. *(Brooklyn: Carlson Publishing, Inc., 1993), p. 441.*

Smith, Jessie Carney, ed. *Notable Black American Women.* Book II (Detroit: Gale Research, 1996), p. 229.

Wina Marché

Dr. Eliza Anna Grier

North Carolina; Former Slave (1864-1902)
Women's Medical College of Pennsylvania - 1897

Dr. Grier, the first Black licensed
    lady doctor in Georgia had a slow
    starting practice; she needed years to grow.

A former slave she died five
    years after medical school graduation;
    little time for growth and innovation.

She made the transition from slavery
    to personhood to medical school,
    an inspiration by any rule.

Sources

Abram, Ruth J., ed. *Send Us a Lady Physician: Women Doctors in America, 1835-1920*. 1st ed. (New York: Hemisphere Publishing Corporation, 1990), p. 110, 112.

Galloway-Wright, Brenda. Hine, Darlene Clark, ed. *Black Women in America: An Historical Encyclopedia.* (Brooklyn: Carlson Publishing Inc., 1993), p. 502.

Sammons, Vivian Ovelton. *Blacks in Science and Medicine.* (New York: Hemisphere Publishing Corporation, 1990), p. 107.

Dr. Halle (Hallie) Tanner Dillon Johnson

Pittsburgh (1864-1901)

First Black Woman Resident Physician at Tuskegee Institute

1891-1894

Women's Medical College of Pennsylvania-1891

She was the first lady doctor to pass

    the Alabama State medical exam.

    She improved health care

    in many cities with her "savoir faire".

Dr. Johnson started a school

    for nurses; a dispensary

    for students and community

    during her stay at Tuskegee.

Her Father was a bishop

    in the A.M.E. Church.

    Artist Henry O. Tanner, her brother.

    They were a family of achievers,

    believers, community relievers.

Sources

Abram, Ruth J. *Send Us a Lady Physician: Women Doctors In America, 1835-1920.* (1st ed, New York: Norton, 1986), p. 110, 114.

Brown, Hallie Q. *Homespun Heroines and Other Women of Distinction.* The Schomburg Library of Nineteenth Century Black Writers. (New York: Oxford University Press, 1988), p. 32-33.

Danett, Sylvia G. L. *Profiles of Negro Womanhood.* (1st ed. 2 vols. Yonkers, New York: Educational Heritage, 1964-66), vol. 1. p. 277

Smith, Jessie Carney. Hine, Darlene Clark, ed. *Black Women In America, An Historical Encyclopedia.* (Brooklyn: Carlson Publishing, Inc., 1993), p. 642-44.

Wina Marché

Dr. Sarah Garland Boyd Jones

Albermarle County, Virginia (d. 1905)
Howard Medical School - 1890
Husband, Dr. Miles Berkley Jones
First Black Lady Physician in Virginia

Sarah left the teaching tradition
    and became practicing physician.
The year was 1893
    that she became a licensee.

Husband was a doctor, too.
    As their medical practice grew
they founded a hospital facility
    that also enhanced nurses' ability.

Virginia, the state, was a bit slow
    to let their race-gender cards go.
In 1905 when she died
    no other had crossed the divide.

Sources

Abram, Ruth J. ed. *Send Us a Lady Physician: Women Doctors in America, 1835-1920*. (New York: Norton, 1st ed., 1986), p. 111.

Galloway-Wright, Brenda. Hine, Darlene Clark, ed. *Black Women in America: An Historical Encyclopedia*. (Brooklyn, New York: Carlson Publishing, Inc., 1993), p. 653-654.

Majors, Monroe. *Noted Negro Women: Their Triumphs and Activities*. (Salem, New Hampshire: Ayer Company Publishing, Inc., 1986), p. 242.

Sammons, Vivian Ovelton, *Blacks in Science and Medicine*. (New York: Hemisphere Publishing Corporation, 1990), p. 139.

Dr. Verina Morton Jones

(1865-1943) Cleveland; South Carolina State Normal School
Women's Medical College of Pennsylvania – 1888
Resident Physician at Rust College
She and Husband (Dr. A. W. Morton) Had Joint Practice in Brooklyn
Second Husband (Emory Jones)

Dr. Jones has several firsts
    behind her name – first
    social service organization
    in Brooklyn to serve Blacks – first
    lady doctor to practice in
    Mississippi. A fighter for human rights;
Dr. Jones fought for good with all her might!

She had a long career in healing
    and helping others;
    again, the first lady doctor –
    also advocated civil rights causes
    in Nassau County,
    in Long Island;
Color her kind, skilled, noble, grand!

Sources

Abram, Ruth J. *Send Us a Lady Physician: Women Doctors in America, 1835-1920I.* (1st ed., New York: Norton, 1986), p. 110, 114, 117.

Who's Who in Colored America: A Biographical Dictionary of Notable Living Persons of Negro Descent in America. (New York: Who's Who in Colored America Corp., 1941-44), p. 303.

Sammons, Vivian Ovelton. *Blacks in Science and Medicine.* (New York: Hemisphere Publishing Corporation, 1990), p. 139.

Sullivan, Otha Richard and Haskins, Jim, general ed., *American Women Scientists & Inventors.* (New York: John Wiley & Sons, Inc., 2002), p. 92.

Dr. Francis M. Kneeland

Tennessee c. 1873

Meharry Medical College 1898 with Honors

Physician; Surgeon; Memphis, Tennessee

She was the sole Black
    lady doctor in the city
    of Memphis, Tennessee.
    She taught at the local
    medical school; she was
    very active and vocal.

Dr. Kneeland, physician, surgeon,
    the doctor of choice for
    many Memphis ladies.
    Kneeland was an ideal
    lecturer, motivator, inspirator,
    dedicated achiever called to heal.

Sources

http://www./library.utmen.edu/HSLBC/history/sib-bi
http://www.newberryorg/general/L3general.html

Jenkins, Earnestine. Hine, Darlene Clark, ed. *Black Women in America: An Historical Encyclopedia.* (Brooklyn: Carlson Publishing Corporation, 1993), p. 682.

Church, Roberta and Ronald Waters. *Nineteenth Century Memphis Families of Color 1850-1900.* (1987).

Hamilton, Green. *The Bright Side of Memphis (1908).*

Dr. Alice Woodby-McKane

Bridgewater, Pennsylvania (1863-1946)
Women's Medical College of Pennsylvania – 1892
Physician

Dr. Alice Woodby-Mckane
    and Dr. Cornelius Mckane
    medical husband and wife
    lead a dedicated life.

They built and shared
    a hospital showing they cared.
    Liberia was the nation
    for this international relation.

They worked with the folk there too,
    with the poor and veterans who
    sought Civil War pensions.
    She was examiner for these intentions.

To improve health and welfare
    she opened a Savannah health care
    center. The doctor believed
    in passing on what one has received.

Sources

Abram, Ruth J., ed. *Send Us a Lady Physician: Women Doctors in America 1835-1920.* (New York: W.W. Norton & Company, 1985), p. 110, 117.

Davis, Marianna W., ed. 2 vols. *Contributions of Black Women in America* (Columbia, SC: Kenday Press, 1981, 1982) vol. 2, p. 366.

Miller, Janet. Hine, Darlene Clark, ed. *Black Women in America: An Historical Encyclopedia* (Brooklyn: Carlson Publishing Co., 1993), p. 1282-1283.

Who's Who in Colored America: A Biographical Dictionary of Notable Living Persons of Negro Descent in America. (New York: Who's Who in Colored America, 1941-1944), p. 347.

Wina Marché

Dr. Ida Gray Nelson

Clarksville, Tennessee (1867-1953)
First African American Woman to
Receive Doctor of Dental Surgery Degree
University of Michigan Dental School (1890)

The several "firsts" Dr. Gray
    had before her name say
that she was a dental pioneer.
    With memories precious and dear
however, some she'd wished to forget
    like memories about that old duet
often called race and gender.
    Either one could be an offender.

Ida was southern, strong, and tough,
    but being first must have been rough.
Many of the medics before her
    had tales of things that could deter.
Dr. Ida, a long way from Tennessee,
    came to U. of M. for her degree.
She practiced dentistry in Cincinnati,
    and Chicago, she was champion
        of patients and community.

Sources

Carwell, Hattie. *Blacks in Science: Astrophysicist to Zoologist.* (Hicksville, New York: Exposition Press, 1977), p. 23.

Dannett, Sylvia G.L. *Profiles of Negro Womanhood.* 1st ed. 2 vols. (Yonkers, New York: Educational Heritage, 1964-1966.), p. 26.

Hine, Darlene Clark, ed. *Black Women in America: An Historical Encyclopedia.* (Brooklyn, New York: Carlson Publishing, Inc., 1993), p. 1316.

Majors, Monroe. *Noted Negro Women: Their Triumphs and Activities.* (Salem, New Hampshire: Ayer Company Publisher, Inc., 1986), p. 241.

Wina Marché

Dr. Caroline Virginia Still Wiley Anderson

Philadelphia, (1848-1919)
Daughter of Philadelphia Abolitionist William Still;
Niece of Noted Physician James Still
Medical College of Pennsylvania- 1878

Dr. Anderson and her second husband
    helped found a school.
    She was principal for thirty-four years
    uniting her medical and teaching careers.

The Lady Doctor had numerous
    community interests and activities.
    Her medical alumni association
    and YWCA's
    she helped organize in the early days.

Sources

Abram, Ruth J. *Send Us a Lady Physician: Women Doctors In America, 1835-1920. (1st ed. New York: Norton, 1986), p. 110-111.*

Dannett, Sylvia G. L. *Profiles in Negro Womanhood.* 1st ed. 2 vols. (Yonkers, N.Y.: Educational Heritage 1964-66), p. 217.

Galloway-Wright, Brenda. Hine, Darlene Clark, ed. *Black Women in America: An Historical Encyclopedia.* (Brooklyn, New York: Carlson Publishing, Inc., 1993), p. 28-29.

Sammons, Vivian Ovelton. *Blacks in Science and Medicine.* (New York: Hemisphere Publishing Corporation, 1990), p. 11.

Wina Marché

Dr. Sarah Parker Redmond

Physician – Abolitionist- Practiced Medicine in Italy (1826-1894)
Santa Maria Nuova Hospital- Florence, Italy – 1871

Sarah's international fight
    for freedom and the right
of Blacks enslaved in this nation
    were part of her heartfelt oration.
Her family's home in Salem, Mass
    was haven for abolitionist enthusiasts.
She practiced medicine twenty years
    in Italy sustaining two careers;
    as a medical healer
    and abolitionist appealer.

Sources

Bolden, Tonya. *African American Women. "The Redmond Women"*.
(Holbrook, Mass.: Adams Media Corporation, 1996.) p. 35-37.
Danett, Sylvia, G.L. *Profiles of Negro Womanhood*. 1st ed. 2 vols.
(Yonkers, New York: Educational Heritage, 1964-66 vol 1), p.
112-113.

Notable American Women. 1607-1950. (Cambridge, Mass.: Belknap Press of Harvard University Press. 1980), p. 136-137.

Wesley, Dorothy Porter. Hine, Darlene Clark, ed. *Black Women in America: An Historical Encyclopedia.* (Brooklyn: Carlson Publishing Corporation, 1993.) p. 973-974; 919, 455, 1312.

Wina Marché

Dr. Susan McKinney Steward

Brooklyn, New York (1847-1918)
New York Medical College 1870 – Valedictorian

She was the nation's third
    Black lady doctor;
    The first in New York State.
    Her goals were to heal and educate.

A school and medical society bear
    her name. A community activist,
    Dr. Steward was a versatile physician
    Black health care was her mission.

Sources

Abram, Ruth J., ed. *Send Us a Lady Physician. Women Doctors in America 1835-1920.* (New York: W.W. Norton & Company, 1985), p. 108, 111, 114, 116-117.

Brown, Hallie Q. *Homespun Heroines and Other Women of Distinction.* (New York: Oxford University Press, Inc., 1988), p. 160-164.

Ganett, Sylvia, G. L. *Profiles of Negro Womanhood.* 1st ed. 2 vols. (Yonkers, New York: Educational Heritage, 1964-66), p. 313.

Seraille, William. Hine, Darlene Clark, ed. *Black Women in America. An Historical Encyclopedia. (Brooklyn: Carlson Publishing, Inc., 1991)*, p. 469, 923, 1109-1112.

Dr. Georgia Esther Lee Patton Washington

Grundy County, Tennessee (1864-1900)
Meharry Medical School
(One of First Two Black Lady Graduates) 1893
Physician; Surgeon

Dr. Washington had
    several medical firsts –
    surgery license in Tennessee;
    lady doctor to graduate
    from Meharry. Africa was her
    choice to relocate.

So, off to Liberia
    as a medical missionary.
    Despite native fatalism
    and patient doubts
    Dr. Washington and
    her remedies were standouts.

Sources

Abram, Ruth J. *Send Us a Lady Physician: Women Doctors in America 1935-1920*. (New York: W.W. Norton & Company, 1985), p. 110.

Bolden, Tonya. *African American Women*. (Holbrook, Mass.: Adams Media Corporation, 1996), p. 98-100.

Miller, Janet. Hine, Darlene Clark, ed. *Black Women in America, An Historical Encyclopedia*. (Brooklyn: Carlson Publishing, Inc., 1993), p. 1231.

Majors, Monroe Alphus. *Noted Negro Women, Their Triumphs and Activities*. (Salem, New Hampshire: Ayer Company Publishing, Inc., 1986), p. 117-121.

Wina Marché

Dr. Ionia Rollin Whipper

Beaufort, South Carolina (1874-1953)
Howard University Medical College – 1903
Physician, Obstetrician, Second Black Resident Physician at
Tuskegee Institute

A champion of mothers who were unwed,
    Ionia was among those who tread,
As lady doctors, the halls of Howard U.
    when their numbers are few.
For forty years in Washington, D.C.
    the community shared the benefits of her degree.
She also traveled the southern states
    helping to lower their mortality rates.

Sources

Abram, Ruth J. ed. *Send Us a Lady Physician: Women Doctors In America, 1835-1920*. 1st edition (New York: Norton, 1986), p. 114.

Logan, Rayford W. and Winston, Michael R., eds. *Dictionary of American Negro Biography*. 1st edition. (New York: Norton, 1983), p. 642-643.

Taylor, Theresa. Hine, Darlene Clark, ed. *Black Women in America: An Historical Encyclopedia* (New York: Carlson Publishing, Inc., 1993), p. 1255-1256.

Sammons, Vivian Ovelton. *Blacks in Science and Medicine.* (New York: Hemisphere Publishing Corporation, 1990), p. 247.

PART EIGHT

LATER LADY INSPIRATORS IN MEDICINE

Dr. Mary E. Britton

Lexington, Kentucky; 1858-1925
Chicago's American Missionary Medical College – 1903
Physician, Activist

Dr. Britton was a popular,
    journalist, a great
    speaker, a writer,
    a teacher, a doctor,
    and justice fighter.

Her medical beliefs
    about life included
    what one should eat;
    what one should do;
    no smoking, alcohol, or meat.

Sources

Founders Day Berea College
http://www.berea.edu/Publications/Alumnus/Win
http://www.womeninKentucky.com/site/healthmed

Smith, Jessie Carney. *Notable Black American Women, Book II.* (New York: Gale Research, 1996), p. 55-56.

Wade-Gayles, Gloria. Hine, Darlene Clark, ed. *Black Women in America: An Historical Encyclopedia.* (Brooklyn: Carlson Publishing Corporation, 1993), p. 167-168.

Dr. Ethelene Jones Crockett

St. Joseph, Michigan (1914-1978)

Jackson Community College; University of Michigan

Howard University School of Medicine

Awards: Physician of the Year-1978-Detroit Medical Society

Howardite of the Year-1972; Nine True Women-

1971 Detroit Free Press

Woman of the Year 1972-Zeta Phi Beta Sorority

Detroit Gynecologist; Obstetrician; Community Activist

Michigan's delayed gender/race

    "first" finds Dr. Crockett in place.

The year was 1952.

    Can you believe it was true?

No Black lady obstetrician

    could claim this medical position.

The same was true for gynecology.

    She was the mother of three;

a devoted judge's wife,

    a leader, and an improver of Detroit life.

Sources

Burton Historical Collection. Detroit Public Library. 1-6-79

Davis, Marianna W., editor. *Contributions of Black Women to America*. (Columbia, South Carolina: Kenday Press, Inc., 1881), p. 386.

Detroit News. Obituary. December 30, 1978.

Gavrilovich, Peter, and McGraw, Bill. *The Detroit Almanac: 300 Years of Life in the Motor City*. (Detroit Free Press, 2000), p. 117.

Jones, Iris Sanderson. "Dr. Crockett honored as Woman of the Year. *Detroit* News. Thursday, March 2, 1972.

Dr. Helen Octavia Dickens

An Inspirator- A Race/Gender Pioneer

Dayton, Ohio- (1909)

Physician; Surgeon; Obstetrician; Gynecologist

University of Illinois - 1934, MD

M.M.S. University of Pennsylvania Graduate School of Medicine

1945

Father was born a Tennessee

    slave. He yearned for a college degree.

He was in love with knowledge and learning.

    He finally satisfied this yearning.

Needless to say his hopes were very high

    for Helen, "the apple of his eye."

His dream for her – *try medicine and succeed.*

    Helen liked the idea and agreed.

When Helen was eight Father died.

    The dreams he dreamed for her, she tried.

She and Mother, undaunted by closed doors,

    were ready for rocky academic shores.

You know she made it to medical school

    but the gender – race thing was still rule.

She didn't pay discrimination any mind.

    Helen wasn't the scary or quitting kind.

Doctors do a residency and internship –

    more times for a "stiff upper lip."

Couldn't stay in medical living quarters.

    No lady doctors allowed, school orders.

Ladies found other places for sleeping-

    no heartaches, no whining, no weeping.

For Helen these were mere distractions.

    She had greater plans for greater actions.

Gynecologist, obstetrician,

    surgeon, wife, mother, physician;

awardee, medical administrator;

    "a first", a volunteer, an educator.

A believer in medical prevention,

    pregnancy education her intention.

Teen pregnancy clinic one solution,

    was a major Dickens contribution.

Dr. Helen Octavia Dickens, liver

    of dreams, a pioneer, a giver,

a role model, an inspirator,

    a worker against odds, a first-rater,

a legacy leaver,

    medical achiever.

Her touch survives,

    in many others' lives.

Sources

Jerrido, Margaret. Hine, Darlene Clark, ed. *Black Women in America: An Historical Encyclopedia.* (*Brooklyn, Carlson Publishing, Inc., 1993*), p. 335-336.

Sammons, Vivian Ovelton. *Blacks in Science and Medicine.* (New York: Hemisphere Publishing Corporation, 1990), p. 74.

Smith, Jessie C. *Notable Black American Women, Book II.* (Detroit: Gale Research, Inc., 1996), p. 179-182.

Who's Who Among Black Americans. (*Northbrook, Illinois*: Who's Who Among Black Americans Publishing Co., 1985). p. 224.

Wina Marché

Dr. Lena Frances Edwards

Washington, D.C. (1900-1986)
Obstetrician; Gynecologist
Howard University College of Medicine – 1924

Dr. Edwards received
   The Presidential Medal
   of Freedom, the highest,
   civilian award in the U.S.,
   for service to the poor.
   She was a legend and more.

She was voted a "Living
   Legend" by Howard U's
   Medical School alumni.
   Her family, patients,
   and friends through the years,
   too, had given grateful cheers.

She and husband, Dr. Keith Madison
   had two doctors among their six
   children, sixteen grandchildren,
   six great grandchildren.
   They are heirs to a legacy honored and great
   history to cherish and perpetuate.

Sources

Ebony. (Chicago; Johnson Publishing Co., February, 1962). p. 59-60; 62; 64; 66; 68.

Hill, Ruth Edmonds, ed. *Women of Courage.* (Radcliffe College, 1984), p. 60.

Smith, Deborah. Hine, Darlene Clark, ed. *Black Women in America: An Historical Encyclopedia.* (Brooklyn: Carlson Publishing Corporation. 1993), p. 387-388.

Jet (Chicago: Johnson Publishing Co., March 11, 1963), p. 42.

Wina Marché

Dr. Effie O'Neal Ellis

Harkinsville, Georgia (b 1913)
University of Illinois College of Medicine, 1950;
NMA*Trailblazer Award;
Physician, Pediatrician, Public Health Specialist

A graduate grant to study
   diseases and parasites
      in Puerto Rico
         sparked her interest
            in medicine. She became
               aware and began her quest.

Medical School graduation found
   her fifth in her class
      of 160 graduates. Her respect
         ever present for learning,
            she continued studying; a love
               for teaching still burning.

Her speaking tours throughout
   the U.S. focused on her goal
      of sharing information
         that affects policy decisions.
            To that end she served

numerous federal divisions.

Dr. Ellis had her share

    of medical firsts.

        Her first "first" was with AMA**

            as the first Black lady physician,

            to hold the Special Assistant

            Health Service position.

*National Medical Association

**American Medical Association

Sources

Ebony, August, 1974. p. 38.

Galloway- Wright, Brenda. Hine, Darlene Clark, eds. *Black Women in America: An Historical Encyclopedia.* (Brooklyn: Carlson Publishing Corporation, 1993), p. 392.

Sammons, Vivian Ovelton. *Blacks in Science and Medicine.* (New York: Hemisphere Publishing Corporation), p. 84.

Wina Marché

Dr. Roselyn Payne Epps

Little Rock, Arkansas; (b. 1930)
Howard University College of Medicine- 1955
Pediatrician; Professor; Administrator; Community Leader

A practicing pediatrician;
    an advocate for children;
    an advocate for the poor.
    Her wisdom has affected
    many organizations to
    which she has been elected.

Her skills have been apparent
    in numerous settings
    in Washington, D.C.
    the U.N. and other
    places she chose to be.

Sources

Black Enterprise. October, 1988. p. 84.

Henderson, Ashyia N. ed., et al. *Who's Who Among African Americans*. (Detroit: Gale Group. Thomson Learning, 2001), p. 394.

Miller, Janet. Hine, Darlene Clark, ed. *Black Women in America: An Historical Encyclopedia.* Brooklyn: Carlson Publishing Corporation, 1993.), p. 397.

Sullivan, Otha Richard and Haskins, Jim, General Editor. *African American Women Scientists & Inventors.* (New York: John Wiley & Sons, Inc., 2002.), p. 92.

Wina Marché

Dr. Edith Mae Irby (Jones)

Conway, Arkansas (1927)

MD University of Arkansas Medical School - 1952

State of Arkansas Declared May 4, 1979 Edith Irby Jones Day;

Physician

Arkansas U's Medical School

    was rather slow

        to let the race card go

            Edith with her MD

                was the first Black to receive this degree.

She used her talent throughout

    Arkansas, her state.

        She shared her great

            leadership qualifications

                with various groups and associations.

Sources

Ebony, May 1986, p. 42.

Jet, May 26, 1986, p. 13.

Morais, Herbert Montfort. *The History of the Negro in Medicine.* (New York Publishers Company, Inc., 1986, p. 137.

National Medical Association. *Journal,* v. 71, October 1979, p. 1025.

Dr. Agnes D. Lattimer

Memphis, Tennessee (b. 1928)
Chicago Medical School – 1954
Only Black Lady Doctor to Hold Top Post in a Major Hospital-
Major City (Chicago 1986); Physician; Pediatrician

Her childhood career goals
    were part of a never changing list-
    doctor, pilot, and pianist.
    According to her press coverage,
    Dr. Lattimer accomplished all three,
    which was Chicago's blessing to be.

Dr. Lattimer, 1986, became
    Chicago's Cook County Hospital chief.-
    administrator. There is the belief-
    that she was the only
    chief by gender and race,
    of such a large medical work place.

Sources

http://www.chicagobusiness.com/cgi-bin/articl
http://www.libmi.edu/ipoii930721.html

Lunardini, Christine A. Hine, Darlene Clark, ed. *Black Women in America: An Historical Encyclopedia.* (Brooklyn: Carlson Publishing Corporation. 1993.), p. 699.

Sammons, Vivian Ovelton. *Blacks in Science and Medicine.* (New York: Hemisphere Publishing Corporation, 1990), p. 147.

Whitaker, Charles. "Cook County's Top Doctor," *Ebony*, September, 1986. p. 44, 46, 48.

Wina Marché

Dr. Helen Marjorie Peebles-Meyers

New York (1915-2002)
First Black Lady Graduate of Wayne State University
Medical School 1943
Detroit Physician; Medical Administrator

Seventy-nine years after
    the first U.S.
        lady doctor's degree
            Dr. Marjorie was another first
                times three.

She was Detroit Receiving
    Hospital's first Black
        lady intern and resident
            in addition
                she was the hospital's first
                    Black Lady Chief Resident Physician.

She retired in 1985
    as Ford Motor
        Chief Physician.
            Hers was a noble sojourn
                of commitment, sharing,
                    involvement, honors, concern.

Sources

Ebony, December 1986. p. 68.

Gavrilovich, Peter and McGraw, Bill, Eds. *The Detroit Almanac: 300 Years of Life In the Motor City*. (Detroit Free Press, 2000), p. 116.

Dr. Marjorie Peebles-Meyers. Obituary (Detroit, *Michigan Chronicle*, January 30-February 5, 2002), p. 3A.

Who's Who Among Black Americans (Norton, Illinois: Who's Who Among Black Americans, Publishing Co., 1975/1976), p. 657.

PART NINE

MODERN LADY INSPIRATORS IN MEDICINE

Dr. Shantwania Buchanan

(1976) Tougaloo College- Magna Cum Laude
MD Brown Medical College 2001-Dean's List
Triumph Over Adversity an Inspiration

Shantwania's grandmother, who was blind,
 strived to cultivate the child's mind.
She taught Shantwania to read at age two.
 Grandmother knew as the child grew
she would need an extra hook;
 So, the Bible became their textbook.
A sharp mind was the hook to pull through
 life's stormy days with skies not so blue.

At the wondrous, carefree age of six years
 she still had Grandmother's love and tears.
Grandmother taught; Shantwantia learned.
 At six she had not discerned
that some lessons were outside the range
 of tasks children do. Such as change
the bedclothes when Granny was sick.
 Shantwania learned to cook; her mind was quick.

When Shantwania was eleven Grandmother died.
 Shantwania acting like "little mother" tried

to be her two siblings' protector

    from life and the foster care specter.

Their home soon became a drug den.

    Mother was there now and then.

And one thing lead to another;

    eviction, things fell apart, no grandmother.

Mother battled old substance abuse

    but one day without a word or excuse,

she walked out; went on her merry way.

    Shantwania was groomed for this day.

While trying to keep the family together

    they became homeless in all kinds of weather.

Their survival against a foster care battle

    was the vow, "Keep quiet and don't tattle!"

There they were 11, 7, and 4,

    hoping no one would know the score.

So, they didn't miss much school

    her survival plan and rule

was to take turns babysitting

    the four year old. Money permitting,

from shooting craps, they'd have motel rent.

    Safety, shelter, and comfort this meant.

She'd watched her mother's friends.

    Her winnings helped to make ends

meet. As her siblings' caregiver

    soon she was a "mule" – drugs to deliver.

At age 11 she thought it the same

    as drug errands for Mother, just a new name.

"Mule" at eleven; errands state to state.

    It upgraded shelter, and the food that they ate.

Siblings "tucked safely" in a motel

    she hoped everything would go well.

They had instructions, and plenty

    stuff to eat, not to open the door for any

person or reason. Things seemed at their best,

    but soon Shantwania was under arrest.

At age 14 she had a court date;

    arrested at home in her own state.

Drug arrest in the neighborhood

    She thought "foster care" not good!

The judge was impressed –A's all- straight

    But foster care still was their fate.

The Judge thought this ruling best

    with her passing each drug free test.

She had several foster care bad starts

    until the Mayweathers' loving hearts.

To the Mayweathers she was a delight
  the relationship was just right.
Shantwania's siblings were nearby.
  Everybody was happy, no need to cry.
Grandmother had said, If you **must** then
  cry and then no more. Then start again.
Homeless times and hunger now the past
  things were getting better at last.

High school and then college was the mission.
  How, where do the poor get tuition?
Shantwania belonged among learning scholars.
  Coca Cola agreed with $20,000.
Concerned folk, angels, and fans cheer.
  She was now able to learn a career.
The Mayweathers, William Winter
  each a well wisher, each a mentor.

The Mayweathers' walls are award filled,
  probably from the training Grandmother instilled.
The awards attest to her focus and drive,
  her strength and will to survive.
Shantwania's life is an old saying come true.
  You can't control what happens to you.
You can't control what happens around you,
  but you can control what you do.

Her two siblings? Sister finished community college.

    Brother joined the marines for service and knowledge.

Shantwania is a medical doctor today

    in spite of the struggle along the way.

Hopefully, her struggle to survive will inspire

    others to keep going and not tire.

The young or old whatever the generation

    have dreams or goals; they too need inspiration.

Sources

English, Bella. "Homeless big sister transforms herself into a MD". *Detroit Free Press*. May 28, 2001. p. 3C.

http://www.brownalumnimagazine.com/storydetai

http://www.bur5relles.com/transcripts/cbs/esho

http://www.umassd.edu/SpecialProgram/obcs/obcsTextll.html

Whitaker, Charles. "From Homelessness to Med School To Medals To Millions" *Ebony*, December, 2001, p. 46-49; 178.

Wina Marché

Dr. Alexa I. Canady

Lansing, Michigan (1950)
University of Michigan Medical School With Honors, 1975
Physician, Pediatric Neurosurgeon
A Modern Day Inspirator

Dr. Canady's career
    is a four times "first";
        first Black U.S. neurosurgeon;
          first lady U.S. neurosurgeon;
            first neurosurgeon resident
              at University of Minnesota;
                first gender/race Chief
                  of Pediatric Surgery
                    Children's Hospital- Detroit
She is a race/gender pioneer.

How? Some things are "a given".
    She was expected to achieve.
      She was encouraged by her family.
        Daddy is a dentist.
          Grandmother was a college professor.
          Mother, besides being a housewife,
            was a college administrator.
              Her three brothers are lawyers.
She was motivated, but not driven.

Well-known and respected,

    according to her mentor,

        she has built Children's

            Hospital into a nationally,

                respected service. This could

                    be predicted, would be expected.

                        Her academic achievement was

                          high from early elementary

                              straight through medical school.

Her competency was expected.

Following her family's ways,

    she has taught

        in higher education;

            the University of Pennsylvania;

                Detroit Henry Ford Hospital;

                    Detroit's Wayne State University.

                    She has many awards

                        in community service

                          despite long hospital hours.

There are some 14 hour days.

In case some one inquires –

    her positive mindset

        is the aura of her inner peace;

is the warmth her patients feel.

is the confidence their family feels.

Her mentoring is grounded

in honesty about choosing medicine;

in honesty about the "hard knocks";

in honesty about the race/gender thing.

Dr. Alexa I. Canady inspires.

Sources

Anstett, Patricia. "Neurosurgeon finds joy in healing." *Detroit Free Press*. March 3, 1999. p. 1A.

Ebony. September, 1983. p. 72-76.

http://www.detnow.com/fromtheheart/000711h.ht

http://www.umich.edu~newsinfo/Releases/1995/

http://www.umich.edu~urecord/9495/Jun19-95/a

Lanker, Brian. *I Dream a World*. (New York: Steward, Tabori, & Chang, Inc., 1989), p. 128.

Dr. Joycelyn Jones Elders

Schall, Arkansas (b. 1933)
University of Arkansas MD - 1960
Physician; Pediatrician; Endocrinologist

Dr. Elders lived the American story –
    from child sharecropper to U.S.
    Surgeon General. Her success
    is a symbol of hope that
    no matter how humble or poor
    one can open any closed door.

Her 1987 appointment
    was Arkansas' historic bid
    to lift the gender and race lid.
    That year Governor Bill Clinton
    appointed Elders State Health Director,
    the people's health care protector.

She is an acclaimed expert
    in juvenile insulin dependent diabetes.
    She is known for research in other diseases.
    Dr. Joycelyn Jones Elders will be remembered
    for the issues she urged America to address
    while she was the "first" Black Surgeon General U.S.

Sources

Cox, Clinton. Haskins, Jim, ed. *African American Healers.* (New York: John Wiley & Sons, Inc., 2000.), p. 232-236.

Friedman, T. "Clinton picks Arkansas official to be new Surgeon General. *The New York Times*, December 15, 1992. p. B11.

Perego, L. "Surgeon General fought hard for youth" *The New York Times* December 14, 1994. p. A22.

Sammons, Vivian Ovelton. *Blacks in Science and Medicine.* (New York: Hemisphere Publishing Corporate, 1990.), p. 83.

Sullivan, Otha Richard. Haskins, Jim, gen. ed. *African American Women Scientists And Inventors.* (New York: John Wiley & Sons, Inc., 2002), p. 92.

Dr. Mae Carol Jemison

Decatur, Alabama (1956); Cornell University Medical School 1981

NASA, Engineer, Astronaut, MD, Professor at Dartmouth College

Scientist; Philanthropist; Speaks Four Languages

Dr. Jemison the "first"
    Black lady NASA astronaut
    is an amazing person.
    She earned a double
    degree from Stanford
    without any trouble.

Engineering and Afro-American
    Studies were the degrees.
    That was 1977.
    1981, four years later
    she received the MD,
    Then her achievements were greater.

In 1985
    it was the Peace Corps,
    as a medical officer in,
    Liberia and Sierra Leone.
    In 1987 her astronaut
    status became known.

Dr. Jemison seeks to
    improve health care
    in West Africa.
    Throughout our nation
    she seeks to increase student interest
    in science and technology education

An amazingly versatile
    lady. Like many of
    the Black lady doctors
    her commitment to health
    care reached another level –
    service became her wealth.
    Her life of service
        and dedication
        is an inspiration.

Sources

Burns, Khephra and Miles, Williams. *Black Stars in Orbit: NASA African American Astronauts*. (San Diego: Gulliver Books-Harcourt Brace & Company, 1996), p. 8-9; 64-67.

http://www.cnn.com/SPECIALS/2002/blackhistor

http://www.starchild.gsfc.nasa.gov/docs/starchild

Lunardini, Christine and Hine, Darlene Clark, ed. A. *Black Women in America: An Historical Encyclopedia.* (Brooklyn, New York: Carlson Publishing, Inc., 1993), p. 633-635.

McKissack, Patricia. McKissack, Frederick. *African American Scientists.* (Brookfield, Connecticut: The Millbrook Press, 1994), 56-59.

Sullivan, Otha Richard, Ed.D. and Haskins, Jim, General Editor. *African American Women Scientists and Inventors.* (New York: John Wiley & Son, Inc., 2002), p. 112-116.

PART TEN

EARLY INVENTORS

David Baker

Inventions: Railway Device; High Water Device; Tire Saver Device
Los Angeles, (1881-19??)

David Baker
   was three
   times a
   patentee.

One Time
   for a high
   water
   device.

One time
   for railway
   signals
   relay.

One time
   for the juncture
   to prevent
   tire puncture.

Much of this
   he learned
   through credits
   earned
   in classes
   at night
   and lessons
   he'd write
   and mail.

Though he
   bought
   the learning above,
   he was mostly
   self-taught.

Sources

Sammons, Vivian Ovelton. *Blacks in Science and Medicine.* (New York: Hemisphere Publishing Corporation, 1990), p. 18.

U. S. Patent Office Microfilm. *David Baker* 1,054,267. February 25, 1913. Great Lakes Patent and Trademark Center. Detroit Public Library.

U. S. Patent Office Microfilm. *David Baker* 1,154,162. September 21, 1915. Great Lakes Patent and Trademark Center. Detroit Public Library.

U. S. Patent Office Microfilm. *David Baker* 1,620,054. March 8, 1927. Great Lakes Patent and Trademark Center. Detroit Public Library.

Henry Baker

c. 1870

Writer, U.S. Patent Office

Henry Baker of the Patent Office U.S.
 did Black inventors' history address.
With his help and the U.S. Commission
 of the 1900 Paris Exposition,
 letters were sent to identify patentees.
They identified 400 Black patent awardees.

350 at the Paris Exposition were displayed.
A base for Black inventors' history was laid.
W.E.B. DuBois helped Thomas J. Calloway
 organize the Black inventors' display.

Thanks to Henry Baker's concern,
 Black inventors' early history is easy to learn.
The U.S. Patent Office and libraries have lists
 of Black inventors who without Baker
 we might have missed!

Sources

Baker, Henry Edwin. *The Colored Inventor: A Record of Fifty Years.* (New York: Crisis Publishing Co., 1913), Revised.

Haskins, Jim. *Outward Dreams: Black Inventors and Their Inventions.* (New York: Walker and Company, 1991), p. 54.

http://www.collectinginsulators.com/Patents-U

http://www.inventors.about.com/library/inventors/

Jeremiah D. Baltimore

Engineer; Machinist; Invented a Pyrometer
Philadelphia (1852-19??)

Jeremiah David Baltimore,
    what did life have in store
    for this little creative boy;
    who liked a pot or pan as a toy?
Mother let him have his fun;
    she didn't stop her creative son.

Folks were often surprised
    by the things he devised;
    like when the young toiler
    fashioned a workable steam boiler
    from parts folk had discarded
    and gave it an engine that started.

His minister was so delighted
    that the community was invited
    when he displayed it at the school.
They probably thought it was "cool",
    If they used words that way
    back in Jeremiah Baltimore's day.

Jeremiah's second time around
 newspapers' praises did abound.
The boiler was taken to the U.S.
 Patent Office. Many it did impress.
So he decided to become an engineer
 Yes, there were roadblocks to his career.

Often he was "the only" and "the first",
 but obstacles didn't quelch his thirst.
With closed doors or a hassle or two
 career goals he continued to pursue.
He is certainly an inspiration
 for folk who need motivation.

He invented a measuring device,
 a pyrometer. It does suffice
 when a temperature is too hot
 for a thermometer to plot a
 reading at extremely high degrees
 the pyrometer reads it with ease.

We're happy Jeremiah D. Baltimore
 had the desire to explore
 his mother's pots and pans
 with his creative mind and hands.
It's good folk helped Baltimore
 by encouraging him to explore.

Sources

Allen-Williams Cheryl, editor. Newton, Kim, researcher. *Pathfinders: Afro-American Achievers and Inventor.* (Detroit: Michigan Consolidated Gas Company, no date.)

Gibbs, C.R. *Blacks Inventors from Africa to America.* (Silver Spring, Maryland: Three Dimensional Publishing Company, 1999), p. 91.

Sammons, Vivian Ovelton. *Blacks in Science and Medicine.* (New York: Hemisphere Publishing Corporation, 1990.), p. 19.

Simmons, William J. *Men of Mark: Eminent Progress and Rising.* (Cleveland, OH: Rewell Publishing Co., 1891.) 736 p. (Reprint. New York: Arno Press, 1968.) p. 1114. Reprint of 1887 edition.

Wina Marché

Andrew Jackson Beard

Inventions – Jenny Coupler; Two Plows; Rotary Engine

Born in Eastlake, Alabama (1849-1921)

Andrew Jackson Beard was
> not an impatient man,
> but three weeks to Montgomery
> by oxen to sell his apples!!

He had fifty bushels to sell.
> Farming wasn't for him!
> He gave it five years.
> Time to try another business.

Flour, everybody needs flour.
> He built his first flour-mill.
> Later he invented a plow;
> got a patent; a $4,000 sale.

Beard invented a second plow;
> He sold this plow patent, too.
> $5,200 was the sale price!
> Not bad for the year 1887!

Beard enjoyed solving problems.

He enjoyed trying new things.

He sold real estate; bought

Land; made money; attained success.

But the trains were calling him,

Beard couldn't resist the call.

Again, Beard saw a problem;

a life threatening problem!

Coupling train cars was the problem.

Joining two moving cars together

sometimes cost lives and lost limbs.

Families had no insurance those days.

Beard worked on a device

that would solve the problem.

Finally, in 1897 he got a patent

for a coupler that was safe.

He sold the patent to a New

York company for $50,000.

He was quite a man! A former

slave who never went to school!

Andrew Jackson Beard left

his mark with four other

patents including a rotary engine;

and money to a Black school.

Sources

Rywell, Martin (chief compiler), and Wesley, Charles H. et al (consulting editors) 10 vols. *Afro-American Encyclopedia.* North Miami, FL.: Educational Publishers, 1974. Vol. 1. p. 216.

Sullivan, Otha Richard, and Jim Haskins, General Editor. *Black Stars; African American Inventors.* New York: John Wiley & Sons, Inc., 1998. p. 39-41.

U.S. Patent Office Microfilm. *Andrew Jackson Beard.* No. 594,059. 1897. Great Lakes Patent and Trademark Center. Detroit Public Library.

U.S. Patent Office Microfilm. *Andrew Jackson Beard.* No. 478,271. 1892. Great Lakes Patent and Trademark Center. Detroit Public Library.

Williams, James C., (compiler). *At Last Recognition in America A Reference Handbook of Unknown Black Inventors and Their Contributions to America.* Chicago: B.C.A. Publishing Corp., c1978. vol. 1, p. 26.

Dr. George Washington Carver

Born in Missouri near Diamond Grove (1864-1943)
Scientist; Researcher; Chemurgist;
Developed Over 300 Peanut Products;
Over 100 Sweet Potato Products

Baby Carver was not free.

His life was not easy.

His father died.

He and his mother were stolen.

She was sold and never found.

He was found sick and weak.

Family now was Jim,

His brother and the Carvers,

Moses and Susan, his wife.

Carver's life was nature and plants.

Young Carver had a good mind

A good mind to learn.

The Carvers taught him to read and write.

He wanted to go to school.

But Blacks couldn't go,

Not in his town.

He wanted to learn; so he had

To leave and live in another town

213

To go to school.

The Carvers let him go.

Ten years old facing a new life

Eight miles away from the Carvers,

A happy boy working and going to school!

Pretty soon he noticed that teacher

Knew little more than he.

It was time to move along

And seek another open door

That would lead to learning more

About the things he didn't know

Like how things grow and why.

So, he left school, hitching

A ride on a wagon train

Headed for Fort Scott, a city,

In Kansas, seeking knowledge.

Each day was a learning day

With the plants, his toys of younger years.

He studied well plants, and sick plants.

Another city another door,

Minneapolis, Kansas – school at last!

He learned his lessons well there.

Despite poverty and city wandering,

High school prepared him well.

Carver was admitted to college.

Highland University in Kansas.

Higher learning, another door opens.

They didn't know he was Black.

The door slammed shut!

When one door closes another opens!

Simpson College, Indianapolis Iowa

Carver started there to study art.

Nature and plants was the call.

Carver went to Iowa Agricultural School.

The next few years brought success

He graduated with honors-1894,

He became assistant botany instructor.

1896 he earned a Masters degree.

In the fields, he loved most,

Botany and agriculture he

Found the answers to some of his

Childhood nature questions.

The same year, another door opens – a letter

From Tuskegee Institute, a new Black college,

From Booker T. Washington, the president.

The message was Carver's people needed him.

He wrote Washington back, "I'm coming."

An open door, two words history is written!

There were tests of Carver's philosophy,

Start where you are and make the best of it.

There were challenges, the agricultural department

Carver was to chair was on paper only.

There was no science laboratory.

There was no science equipment.

There was little or no money.

There was very poor farming soil.

There were farmers who needed help.

There were students waiting to share his gift.

Carver asked for one room for his laboratory.

He salvaged discarded items; gave them a new use.

He took pots, pans, anything he could find

He made science equipment out of them.

With a mule drawn moveable classroom

Carver shared is knowledge and research

With the farmers and students. They learned

Soil rotation and the benefits of the peanut

For nutrition for both the body and the soil.

He freed them from cotton driven farming;

He freed them from cotton driven economy.

The farmers took his advice and grew peanuts.

Soon they had more peanuts than customers.

Carver showed them many peanut products.

Foreign peanuts began to compete for peanut dollars.

The United Peanut Growers Association

Asked Carver to address Congress about

The problem. He did. He showed them

Many products made from peanuts.

The result of his address was inclusion

Of the peanut as a protected product

In the Hawley-Smoot Tariff Bill.

Carver brought the farmers relief.

Peanuts became a healthy, industry.

Over three hundred peanut products;

Over one hundred sweet potato products.

Over five hundred dyes from twenty-eight plants.

Carver seldom sought patents, although, he had three.

Before 1923 the U. S. Patent Office seldom gave plant patents.

People from around the world sought his advice. He gave it freely.

Dr. George Washington Carver's nearly eighty

Earthly years were years of caring and sharing;

Years of seeing beyond limitations, beyond closed doors.

Him tombstone says it well;

He could have added fortune to fame

But caring for neither,

He found happiness and honor in being helpful to the world.
Haskins, p. 71.

Sources

Haber, Louis. *Black Pioneers of Science and Invention.* (San Diego: Odyssey Book Harcourt Brace & Company, 1970), p. 104-121.

Haskins, Jim. *Onward Dreams Black Inventors and Their Inventions.* (New York: Bantam Books: 1992), p. 63-71.

Hayden, Robert C. *7 African American Scientists.* (New York: Twenty-first Century Books; 1992), p. 110-127.

Yount, Lisa. *Black Scientists.* (New York: Facts on File, 1991), p. 14-27.

J. M. Certain

Invention- A Parcel Carrier for Bicycles
Tampa, Florida; 1899

For certain
    cycling was one
    of J.M.'s pleasures.
    but carrying things
    was a burden.

So, J. M. took
    certain measures;
    a parcel carrier
    J.M. invented.
    then it was
    "take and brake"
    wherever, contented
    be it fragile
        or
    "shake
        and bake".

Sources

An African American Bibliography: Science, Medicine, and Allied Fields; Selected Sources from the Collections of the New York State Library Patents.

Ploski, Harry A. and Williams, *Negro Almanac: A Reference Work on the Afro-American* James. 4th edition. (New York: Wiley, 1983), *p. 1107-1114.*

U. S. Patent Office Microfilm. *J. M. Certain* Number 639, 708. December 26, 1899. Great Lakes Patent and Trademark Center, Detroit Public Library.

Alfred L. Cralle

Invented an Ice Cream Mold and Disher
Pittsburgh, PA - 1897

If you have a "sweet tooth"
    and calories you do not dread;
    I kid you not; it's the truth
    you'll love the invention by Alfred.

He apparently believed in "presentation"
    the art of making food look good;
    the food's look is an invitation
    for you to eat more than you should!

He invented a dish and mold
    to give ice cream a nice shape.
His invention was twofold
    It gave a shape with a scrape.

Sources

U.S. Patents by African Americans. *An African American Bibliography: Science, Medicine, and Allied Fields; selected from the collections of the New York State Library. January, 1991. p. 9.*

U.S. Patent Office Microfilm. *Alfred L. Cralle*. 576,395. February 2, 1897. December 8, 1896. Great Lakes Patent And Trademark Center. Detroit Public Library. Detroit, Michigan.

George Crum *

Creator of Potato Chips; Saratoga Chips
At Moon's Lake House Restaurant
c. 1853; Saratoga Springs, New Jersey

Where did the chip
    potato chip, that is,
    come from?
England had the name
    chip, maybe even the dip;
    George Crum
    is where potato
    chips come from!

Crum was part Black,
    part Native American.
It seems a patron sent back
    fried potatoes to be redone.
Crunchy was the request.
Crum did his angry best!
He did, **thin, and crunchy**
    hard, dry, and munchy!

Much to Crum's surprise
    the patron was delighted!

Wina Marché

Cook Crum didn't realize
   his actions would be cited
   when historians explore
   as potato chip folklore
   his anger and sarcasm
   and the patron's enthusiasm.

In this 1853 setting
   Saratoga Springs was hopping!
Folk wouldn't be forgetting!
Well, Saratoga chips talk wasn't stopping!.
In this garden green state
   the restaurant became a hot dinner date –
   Saratoga chips *at Moon's Lake House*.
Crum was happy and didn't grouse!

Crum's Saratoga chips fame
   helped him get his own place.
Crum's House was the name,
   with charm, love, and grace
   customers could eat chips there.
Oh, they ate them everywhere
   when they took them out
   spreading the word all about!

Crum's anger and later pride,

    Saratoga Chips, are well-known

    worldwide as potato chips.

We can eat them by themselves

    or with food on the side,

    or right from the grocery shelves.

Chips makers are usually local

    where folk are loyal, but vocal.

Would you believe, in a 100-years span

    after Crum there were hot disputes

    about chips sold in a can.

There were even chips lawsuits!

Folk thought the name abused.

The word "chips" they wished used

    only when they were in a bag.

Chips in a can meant red flag!

Do you like them in a can?

Are you routing for chips in a bag?

"Cause you're an old time fan?

Do you sometimes brag,

    "Any can, any bag, any day

    at home, at school or play

    that you willingly raise a voice

    not to fret about the choice,

Wina Marché

but to joyously admit

you never eat one and quit?"

Sources

Gibbs, C.R. *Black Inventors from Africa to America.* (Silver Spring, Maryland: Three Dimensional Publishing Company, 1999), p. 87.

Harmon, John E. *Atlas of Popular Culture in Northeastern United States.*

http://www.geography.ccsu.edu/harmonj/atlas/potchips.htm

Panati, C. *Panati's Extraordinary Origin of Everyday Things.* (New York: Perennial Library, 1989), p. 388.

Samuel, P. *Chipping Away at the Champ.* Forbes, April 25, 1994. p. 107-116.

Saunders, Doris E. ed. *The Ebony Handbook by the Editors of Ebony.* (Chicago: Johnson Publication Co., 1974), p. 371.*

Snack Food Association. *50 Years A Foundation for the Future.* Alexandria, VA: Snack Food Association.

http://www.sfa.org/history1.html

"What Began As a Joke".

http://www.geography.ccsu.educ/harmonj/atlas/potchips.htm

*Ebony Handbook lists inventor's name as Hyram S. Thomas

226

David A. Fisher, Jr.

Invention – Furniture Caster
Washington, D.C.; 1876

David A Fisher invented a device
    he called a furniture caster.
It was three times nice.
    One, it moved things faster.
Two, it could prevent disaster.
    Three, it was easy to master.
That it was useful all agreed;
    and certainly there was a need!

Sources

Sammons, Vivian Ovelton. *Blacks in Science and Medicine*. (New York: Hemisphere Publishing Co., 1990), p. 91.

U.S. Patent Office Microfilm. *David A. Fisher* Patent Number 174,794. March 14, 1876. Great Lakes Patent and Trademark Center. Detroit Public Library.

Williams, James C. (compiler) *At Last Recognition in America: A Reference Handbook of Unknown Black Inventors and Their Contributions to America*. (Chicago: B.C.A. Publishing Corp., 1978), p. 6.

Wina Marché

Dr. Virgil Arnett Gant

Pharmacologist; Invented – Chemicals for Hair
Oak Park, Illinois (1897-19??)

Dr. Gant's field of expertise
    was pharmacology.
He could discuss with ease
    a medicine's quality
    its long term effect
    and what one could expect.

Healthy hair was another concern.
    What a blessing for hair care.
His invention helped folk to learn
    how to be safe and still have flair.
In 1957, '56 and three
    he was three times a patentee.

Sources

Sammons, Vivian Ovelton, *Black in Science and Medicine.* (New
    York: Hemisphere Publishing Corporation, 1990), p. 97

U.S. Patent Microfilm. *Virgil Arnett Gant* 2,643,375. June 23, 1953. Great Lakes Patent and Trademark Center. Detroit Public Library.

U.S. Patent Microfilm. *Virgil Arnett Gant.* 2,750,947, June 19, 1956. Great Lakes Patent and Trademark Center. Detroit Public Library.

U.S. Patent Microfilm. *Virgil Arnett Gant.* 2,787,274. April 2, 1957. Great Lakes Patent and Trademark Center. Detroit Public Library.

Wina Marché

Dr. George F. Grant

b. 1800s; Inventor of Cleft Palate Corrective Device
Inventor of the Golf Tee; Boston Dentist; DDS. Harvard 1870
Harvard Dental School Professor; Cleft Palate Expert;

Golfer, dentist, Dr. G.F.G.
    earned a Harvard dental degree.
    Then he took one step more
        and opened another academic door
            by teaching at Harvard's Dental School,
            thereby breaking an unwritten rule.

Dr. G's cleft palate disorder expertise
    helped patients speak clearly with ease.
        Being a golf devotee Dr. G.
            invented the sandless golf tee,
                a wooden peg, a rather small thing
                    that changed the serious golfer's swing.

Imagine this everyday ancient scene:
    golfers trying to be focused and serene
        carrying large boxes of wet sand
            for making a sand tee by hand.
                This was devotion, would you agree?
                It was time for a tee by Dr. G.!

The game of golf has not been the same
since Dr. G. improved his own game
with a new wooden tee design
and received a patent in 1899.
Now thanks to young, champion Tiger Woods
the tee is known in many neighborhoods.

Sources

Gibbs, C.R. *Black Inventors from Africa to America*. (Silver Spring, Maryland: Three Dimensional Publishing Company, 1999), p. 103, 232.

Hayden, Robert C. *II African American Doctors*. (Frederick, MD.: Twenty-First Century Books, 1992), p. 16.

Sammons, Vivian Ovelton. *Blacks in Science and Medicine*. (New York: Hemisphere Publishing Corporation, 1990), p. 104.

U.S. Patent Office Microfilm. *George F. Grant*. No. 638,920. December 12, 1899. Great Lakes Patent and Trademark Center. Detroit Public Library. Detroit, Michigan.

Wina Marché

Augustus Jackson

Created Ice Cream
Philadelphia, 1832

Around the history
      of ice cream
      there is some mystery.
It does seem
      that historians are creative
      and rather dramatic
      not always educative,
      thus creating static.

But this we know to be
      true that a man whose name
      was Jackson was the key
      to culinary fame
      with the discovery of ice cream
      in the city of Philly
      where vendors did scream,
      sing, and chant willy, nilly.

Let's get back to Jackson.
      One day by accident
      busy and on the run,

a new dessert he did invent.

While chilling cream with ice

he found he had **iced cream**!

Jackson tasted and thought, "Nice!"

Friends thought it superb, supreme!

Augustus, his first name,

Philadelphians knew.

Iced cream was his business game

He made more and business grew.

His vendors' businesses did too.

Black vendors prospered well.

Before Jackson was through

He was wealthy, pray tell!

Things were fine; life was swell!

For Augustus

we should

suggest knighthood,

offer to serenade;

give a parade;

call the brigade;

so all will know

we scream;

we scheme;

we dream

233

Wina Marché

of ways
to eat ice cream
and keep
a physique
supreme!

Source

http://inventors.about.com/library/inventors/blicecream.htm

http://www.inventorsmuseum.com/icecream.htm

Ploski, Harry and Williams, editors and compilers. *The Negro Almanac: A Reference Work on the Afro American*, 4th ed. (New York: Wiley, c1983.), p. 1056.

Saunders, Doris E. editor. *Ebony Handbook by the Editors of Ebony*. (Chicago: Johnson Publishing Co., 1974), p. 371.

Spradling, Mary Mace, ed. *In Black and White: A Guide to Magazine Articles, Newspaper Articles and Books Concerning More than 15,000 Black Individuals and Groups. 3rd* edition 2 vols. (Detroit: Gale Research Co., c1980), p. 478.

234

Daniel Johnson

Kansas City, Missouri; c. 1800s
Inventions: Lawn Mower Attachment; Grass Receiver;
Revolving Dining Table

Daniel Johnson had patents three.
    Before his patents folk longed to see
    a neat lawn without a backache.
It was the grass they cut and then rake.
    Daniel's idea did come to pass
    then gathering up the grass
    was more like child's play.
His invention did both along the way.

This information may seem unbelievable
    and even inconceiveable.
Daniel couldn't read or write
    but had the inventor's light.
He didn't need to be a rocket
    scientist to know his work docket
    needed a "re-arrange"
    or some type of change!

Sources

Inventor Online Museum.
http://www.inventorsmuseum.com/djohnson.htm

U.S. Patents by African Americans. An African American Bibliography: Science, Medicine, and Allied Fields; Selected Sources from the Collections of the New York State Library. January, 1991. p. 10.

U.S. Patent Microfilm. *Daniel Johnson.* No. 369,089. January 15, 1889. Great Lakes Patent & Trademark Center. Detroit Public Library.

U.S. Patent Microfilm. *Daniel Johnson.* No. 410,836. September 10, 1889. Great Lakes Patent & Trademark Center. Detroit Public Library.

U.S. Patent Microfilm. *Daniel Johnson.* No. 429,629. June 10, 1890. Great Lakes Patent & Trademark Center. Detroit Public Library.

Annie Turnbo Malone

1869-1957; Metropolis, Illinois

Inventor, Entrepreneur- Hair Products- Poro School

Annie Turnbo Malone,

    her business was hair care.

She set the styling tone

    for the 20's hair flair.

Madame Walker was her student

    but considered independence prudent.

At some point Malone

    had 75,000 folk

    selling, working on their own.

For Malone there was a yoke,

    both personal and financial,

    the damage to her was substantial.

14 million dollars at one time.

    Malone married and shared

    at her company's prime.

Her giving showed she cared.

    She received much and gave much.

Many lives she was able to touch.

Sources

Bolden, Tonya. *The Book of African American Women*. (Holbrook, Massachusetts: Adams Media Corporation, 1996), p. 170-171.

Brodie, Michael James. *Created Equal: The Lives and Ideas of Black American Innovators*. (New York: William Morrow and Company, Inc., 1993), p. 119-120.

Sullivan, Otha Richard. Haskins, Jim. General Editor. *African American Women Scientists & Inventors*. (New York: John Wiley and Sons, 2002), p. 31-34, 43.

Benjamin Montgomery

A Slave; Invented a Boat Propeller; Managed a Cotton Plantation;
Became Wealthy;
Father of Isaiah Founder of a Mississippi Town That Is Now Mound
Bayou

Benjamin Montgomery around 1850
Knowing that a boat can be shifty
Invented a propeller for a boat
That was improved to keep it afloat
Now, there is more to Benjamin's story.
There were trials, triumphs, and glory.
A slave in body, but not in mind
He would read everything he could find.

Sold to Joseph Davis at seventeen
He ran away – *split the slave scene.*
To remain a slave was not his intent.
Davis realized Benjamin's restless bent.
He let Benjamin use his library.
This practice was extraordinary.
It was obvious Ben wanted to learn
And Davis had another concern.

He had a plan, an utopian dream
Of him, Ben, and the slaves as a team-
A "community of cooperation" –
Even a model slave plantation.
This was Joseph Davis' dream, his plan.
Ben liked the idea and said, "I can".
Ben was creative and reliable.
Davis' brother thought the plan not viable.

Jefferson and Joseph- heirs to the land,
Davis Bend, now under their command.
Ben managed Davis Bend plantation
With results beyond expectations.
Living needs were met, treatment was fair.
Slaves even had health and dental care.
Despite it all, they still were not free.
Davis Bend was a model to see.

Then came Civil War, Freedom, and Change.
In that order did things rearrange.
The Davis men left their experiment.
One became the south's president.
Freedom – Joseph's plan got a new start.
Ben, now landowner, with Joseph's part.
Joseph and Benjamin made a deal
That for Ben had success appeal.

Ben found success in the market place.

News coverage often forget his race.

Ben became very wealthy as well.

Joseph's family enjoyed Ben's "rich spell".

Toward Ben's death things began to fail.

Jefferson never approved the sale;

So, he foreclosed when he got the chance;

But history was made despite his stance.

Ben's story continued ten years later;

Reborn with a success that was greater

When two cousins settled

a prosperous Black town,

Mound Bayou, Mississippi, -

of national renown.

A town of landowners,

"a community of cooperation";

A town of pride:

a town of inspiration.

No, Benjamin Montgomery's

story was not done.

The settlers were Ben's nephew,

Benjamin T. Green,

and Isaiah Montgomery,

Benjamin Montgomery's son!

Sources

Burnham, Philip. "Paradoxical Plantation". *American Legacy*. (New York: RJR Communications and American Heritage, a Division of Forbes, Inc., Spring, 1998, vol. 4, no. 1), p. 42-46; 48-50.

Franklin, John Hope. Moss, Alfred, Jr. *From Slavery to Freedom*. (New York: McGraw Hill. 7th Edition, 1994), p. 133.

Hermann, Janet Sharp. *The Pursuit of a Dream*. (New York: Oxford University Press, 1981, p. 109-216; 219-245.

Sullivan, Otha Richard. Haskins, Jim, general editor. *African American Inventors*. (New York: John Wiley & Sons, Inc., 1998), p. 20-24.

Robert Pelham

Detroit, Michigan (1859-1943)
Inventor – Tabulating Machine; Pasting Machine

Robert Pelham was a patentee
   with ideas totaling three.
He had several careers;
   the Census Bureau, written ideas-
the newspaper, *Post*.
   The Plain Dealer was foremost.

Inventions – a – tabulating machine
   for manufacturers' census routine.
A tallying machine for population
   division and configuration;
A pasting machine, an innovation,
   another Pelham family revelation.

Sources

Garilovich, Peter and McGraw, Hill. *The Detroit Almanac: 300 Years of in the Motor City.* (Detroit: The Detroit Free Press, 2001), p. 252.

Gibbs, C.R. *Black Inventors from Africa to America.* (Silver Spring, Maryland: Three Dimensional Publishing Company, 1999), p. 181-184.

McRae, Shirley McTyre, and McRae, Norman. *The First City of the Midwest.* (Carlsbad, CA.: Heritage Media Corporation, 2001), p. 59.

U.S. Patent Office Microfilm. *Robert Pelham.* No. 807,685. December 19, 1905. Great Lakes Patent and Trademark Center. Detroit Public Library. Detroit.

Sammons, Vivian Ovelton. *Blacks in Science.* (New York: Hemisphere Publishing Corporation, 1990), p. 187.

William B. Purvis

Inventor-Sixteen Patents Between 1882-1897
   Philadelphia

Busy inventor William B. Purvis
   was very talented and not nervous
   about sharing his inventive skill.
With sixteen patents call him versatile!

Ten patents of Purvis' sixteen
   were for a paper bag machine.
William's other patents were six,
   including a pen, quite a mix!

It seems when he saw a need,
   solving the problem was his creed.
No matter the size large or small
   William B. Purvis tackled them all.

Sources

Gibbs, C.R. *Black Inventors from Africa to America.* (Silver Spring, Maryland: Three Dimensional Publishing Company, 1999), p. 91.

U. S. Patents by African Americans. An African American Bibliography: Science, Medicine, and Allied Fields; Selected Sources from the Collection of the New York State Library. January, 1991, p. 13.

U. S. Patent Office Microfilm. *William B. Purvis*. Patent No. 419,065. January 7, 1890. Great Lakes Patent and Trademark Center. Detroit Public Library. Detroit, Michigan.

U.S. Patent Office Microfilm. *William B. Purvis*. Patent No. 420,099. January 28, 1890. Great Lakes Patent and Trademark Center. Detroit Public Library. Detroit, Michigan.

U.S. Patent Office Microfilm. *William B. Purvis*. Patent No. 519,291 May, 1, 1894. Great Lakes Patent Center Trademark Center. Detroit Public Library. Detroit, Michigan.

Lloyd P. Ray

Invented- an Industrial Dust Pan
1897 – Seattle, Washington

Everyday thoughts and everyday things
    are stuff of which inventions are made;
    our needs or those of queens and kings;
    things we desire or things that aid.

When will we need a pan;
    like Ray's pan for dust?
Clean and sweep all we can
    to lift the dust a pan is a must!

Sources

Negro Almanac: A Reference Work on The African American. (Detroit: Gale Research, Inc., Fifth Edition, 1989), p. 1112.

U. S. Patent Office Microfilm. *Lloyd P. Ray.* Patent No. 587,607. August 3, 1897. Great Lakes Patent and Trademark Center. Detroit Public Library.

Wina Marché

Judy V. Reed

Washington, D.C.
First U.S. Black Lady Patent Holder 1884;
Invented a Dough Rolling and Kneading Device

1884 patent holder Judy's
    dough making duties
    were much simplified
    when she applied
    the use of her invention.
Its time saving intention,
    dough rolling and kneading
    helped heavy duty feeding.

1884 was the year
    of her culinary gear.
It is well understood
    patentee Sarah Goode
    and her folding bed
    became the "second" instead;
    invented in the 1885's
    in the gender/race archives.

Sources

U.S. Patent Office Microfilm. *Judy Reed*. No. 305,474. September 23, 1884. Great Lakes Patent & Trademark Center. Detroit Public Library. Detroit.

U.S. Patent Office Microfilm. *Sarah Goode*. No. 322,177. July 14, 1885. Great Lakes Patent & Trademark Center. Detroit Public Library. Detroit.

Wina Marché

Humphrey H. Reynolds

Porter for Pullman Railroad Sleeping Cars
Invented – Train Window Ventilator; Bridge Safety Gate
  1880s- Detroit, MI.

Humphrey H. Reynolds' idea
  Mr. Pullman liked a lot,
  but made it pretty clear
  "Thank you" was all it got!

So, Reynolds with patent number one
  went to court to right the wrong.
  10,000 were the dollars he won!
So, Pullman sang a different song!

Reynolds had another patent, too,
  for a bridge safety gate.
  This time he didn't need to sue.
October 7, 1890 was his patent date.

Sources

Sullivan, Otha Richard and Jim Haskins, General Editor. *African American Inventors*. (New York: John Wiley & Sons, Inc., 1998), p. 42.

U.S. Patents by African Americans. An African American Bibliography: Science, Medicine and Allied Fields. (New York: New York State Library, January, 1991), p. 13.

U.S. Patent Office Microfilm. *Humphrey H. Reynolds*. 275,271. April 3, 1883. Great Lakes Patent and Trademark Center. Detroit Public Library. Detroit.

U.S. Patent Office Microfilm. *Humphrey H. Reynolds*. 437,937. October 7, 1890. Great Lakes Patent & Trademark Center. Detroit Public Library. Detroit.

Wina Marché

A. L. Rickman

Invention – Overshoe; Forerunner of Rubbers for Shoes
Scio, Ohio (1800s)

The intention
of Rickman's
  invention
      was
        to
        try
        to
        keep
        your
        shoes
        dry.

As a
  matter
      of
      fact
      it
      did
      just
      that!

Source

Negro Almanac: A Reference Work on The African American.
(Detroit: Gale Research, Inc., Fifth Edition, 19889), p. 1112.

U. S. Patent Office Microfilm. *A. L. Rickman.* Patent Number
598,816. February 8, 1898. Great Lakes Patent & Trademark
Center, Detroit Public Library. Detroit.

Samuel R. Scottron

New York – c. 1800s
Invented Window Appliances

Samuel R. Scottron's fame
    came from two types of dressings
    that didn't share the same name,
    though they both were blessings.

Barber Scottron dressed men's hair.
    Inventor Scottron dressed home windows.
The first followed men's fashion flair.
    The second solved ladies' curtain woes.

Samuel's household invention
    to housewives' delight
    ended an old convention
    they were glad to make right!

They gave a sigh of relief.
    No worry about too low
    a curtain line; no hammer grief,
    no nailing curtains to the window.

Samuel's nifty curtain rod

   was accepted with acclaim.

It got the ladies' approval nod

   for no window dressing strain!

Sources

http://www.inventorsmuseum.co/scottron.htm

U.S. Patent Office Microfilm. *Samuel R. Scottron.* No. 224,732. February 17, 1880. Great Lakes Patent and Trademark Center. Detroit Public Library. Detroit.

U.S. Patent Office Microfilm. *Samuel R. Scottron.* No. 270,851. January 16, 1883. Great Lakes Patent and Trademark Center. Detroit Public Library.

U.S. Patent Office Microfilm. *Samuel R. Scottron.* No. 349,525. September 21, 1886. Great Lakes Patent and Trademark Center. Detroit Public Library. Detroit.

Wina Marché

John Stanard

Invented a Refrigerator
1889 - Newark, N.J.

In the year eighteen eighty-nine
    J. Stanard decided to design
    a food cooler with compressed air
    and ether to improve food care.
His refrigerator that year
    made him a design pioneer.

Sources

Sammons, Vivian Ovelton. *Blacks in Science and Medicine.* (New York: Hemisphere Publishing Co., 1990), p. 220.

U.S. Patent Office Microfilm. *J. Stanard.* No. 455,891. July 14, 1889. Great Lakes Patent and Trademark Center. Detroit Public Library.

U.S. Patent Office Microfilm. *J. Stanard.* No. 413,869. 1889. Great Lakes Patent and Trademark Center. Detroit Public Library.

Williams, James C. compiler. *At Last Recognition in America: A Reference Handbook of Unknown Black Inventors and Their Contributions to America.* (Chicago: B.C.A. Publishing Corp., 1978), vol. 1, p. 23.

Thomas W. Stewart

Detroit; b. 1800s
Invented a Mop

Before eighteen ninety-three
    cleaning the kitchen floor
    was on hand and bended knee.
Stewart thought it should be more
    than plop,
        drop,
            sop!
So he invented a mop
    to clean while standing,
    making cleaning less demanding!

Sources

Negro Almanac: A Reference Work on The African American.
(Detroit: Gale Research, Inc., Fifth Edition, 1989), p. 1113.

Saunders, Doris E. ed. *The Ebony Handbook by the Editors.*
(Chicago: Johnson Publication Co., 1974), p. 371.

U. S. Patent Office Microfilm. *Thomas W. Stewart.* Patent Number
499,402. June 13, 1893. Great Lakes Patent and Trademark
Center. Detroit Public Library. Detroit, Michigan.

H. C. Webb

Invention: Engine Powered Farm Implement
  Born in Columbus Town, N.C., 1864

H.C. Webb did invent
    a farm implement.
    I'm sure farmers adored
    and were able to afford
    his palmetto grubbing machine.
It was fast, clean, and routine.

The unwanted palmetto plant
    was abundant never scant.
The Webb Palmetto Grubbing Machine
    could outdo ten men at the scene
    where palmetto leaves had spread,
    threatening crops at the homestead.

This was just one invented device.
    H. C. invented useful machines twice.
With likely career changes ahead
    H.C. chose a new homestead,
Parish, Florida, the new address
    where he pursued business success.

Sources

Pathfinders II. *Afro-American Scientists and Inventors*. Allen Williams, Cheryl, Newton, Kim, researcher. (Detroit: Michigan Consolidated Gas Co.) No Date.

U.S. Patent Office Microfilm. *H. C. Webb*. No. 1,226,425. May 15, 1917. Great Lakes Patent and Trademark Center. Detroit Public Library.

Wina Marché

John T. White

1896 – New York, N.Y.
Invented a Lemon Squeezer

With John T. White's
    device
    we can
    get our
    own
    fresh
    juice.

    We
    can
    squeeze
    more
    than
    twice
    and
    produce
    more
    juice
    for
    use.

Sources

Negro Almanac: A Reference Work On The African American. (Detroit: Gale Research, Inc., Fifth Edition, 1989), p. 1114.

U.S. Patent Office Microfilm. *John T. White.* No. 572,849. December 8, 1896. Great Lakes Patent and Trademark Center. Detroit Public Library. Detroit.

Francis J. Wood

Invented a Potato Digger in 1895
   Greenville, Michigan

Did
   people's
   potato
   cravings
   trigger

a
   need
   to
   make
   the
   harvest
   bigger?

Is
   that
   why
   Wood
   invented
   a
   potato
   digger?

Sources

African American Inventors: Agriculture Related Patents http://www.na/.usda.gov/outreach/patents.pdf

U.S. Patent Office Microfilm. *Francis J. Wood.* No. 537,953. April 23, 1895. Great Lakes Patent & Trademark Center. Detroit Public Library. Detroit.

Wina Marché

Dr. Louis Tompkins Wright

Born in LaGrange, GA (1891-1952)
Invented a Neck Brace and Metal Plate for Splinting
Physician; Surgeon; Civil Rights Activist
MD Harvard 1915- Fourth in His Class

His sixty-one years were
    filled with challenges,
    achievements, firsts, causes
    commitment, and inspiration.

Dr. Louis T. Wright was
    a scholar who graduated
    fourth in Harvard Medical
    School's class of 1915.

When a task was named
    Dr. Wright undertook it with
    all the insight, energy,
    and determination needed.

Dr. Wright invented a neck
    brace; a device for splinting
    (used with broken limbs);
    and disease testing methods.

His *firsts* include New York City
    Municipal Hospital
    appointment as Police Surgeon;
    use of "wonder drug".

His honors include the NAACP
    Spingarn Award in 1940;
    memberships include
    selected Medical Societies.

Along with being a "Mighty
    Medicine Man", Dr. Wright
    was the proud father of two
    accomplished medical women.

Sources

Cox, Clinton. Haskins, Jim, general editor. *African American Healers.*
    (New York: John Wiley & Sons, Inc., 2000), p. 87-93.

Hayden, Robert C. *II African American Doctors.* (New York:
    Twenty-First Century Books, 1992), p. 52-70.

Mabunda, L. Mplo, editor. *The African American Almanac.* (New
    York: Gale Research, 1997), p. 1059.

Matney, William C. *Who's Who Among Black Americans.* (Lake Forest, Illinois: Educational Communications, Inc., 1985), p. 166.

Sammons, Vivian Ovelton. *Blacks in Science and Medicine.* (New York: Hemisphere Publishing Corporation, 1990), p. 259.

PART ELEVEN

LATER INVENTORS

Dr. Robert Gordon Bayless

Yellow Springs, Ohio; National Cash Register Company-Staff
Inventor – a Type of Carbonless Paper;
Six Patents

Dr. Bayless' invention is about a process;
  microencapsulation.
It has possibilities that are limitless.
  Carbon paper was the first application.
Bayless has patents, diverse
  for things in the universe.

Sources

McKissack, Patricia. and McKissack, Frederick. *African American Inventors*. (Brookfield, Connecticut: Millbrook Press, 1994), p. 90.

U.S. Patent Office Microfilm. *Robert Gordon Bayless*. No. 3,565,818. February 23, 1971. U.S. Patent and Trademark Center. Detroit Public Library. Detroit.

U.S. Patent Office Microfilm. *Robert Gordon Bayless*. No. 4,107,071. August 15, 1978. U.S. Patent and Trademark Center. Detroit Public Library. Detroit.

U.S. Patent Office Microfilm. *Robert Gordon Bayless*. No. 3,922,373. November 25, 1975. U.S. Patent and Trademark Center. Detroit Public Library. Detroit.

U.S. Patent Office Microfilm. *Robert Gordon Bayless*. No. 4,073,946. February 14, 1978. U.S. Patent and Trademark Center. Detroit Public Library. Detroit.

U.S. Patent Office Microfilm. *Robert Gordon Bayless*. No. 6,229,140. December 21, 1971. U.S. Patent and Trademark Center. Detroit Public Library. Detroit.

Bertha Berman

Forest Hills, N.Y.
Invention-A Fitted Bed Sheet 1959

It's a treat
    to slide
    into bed
    on a nice
    smooth
    sheet.

Bertha's
    fitted design
    is a blessing
    for folk
    who find
    bed dressing
    rather distressing.

Sources

An African American Bibliography: Science, Medicine, and Allied Fields; Selected Sources from the Collections of the New York State Library. January, 1991, p. 10.

U.S. Patent Office Microfilm. *Bertha Berman.* No. 2,907,055. October 6, 1959. Great Lakes Patent and Trademark Center. Detroit Public Library. Detroit.

Otis Boykin

1920-1982; Dallas, Texas; Fisk University;
Chicago, Illinois; Illinois Institute of Technology;
Inventions: Device Used in Guided Missiles;
Device Used in IBM Computers;
Twenty-six Other Electrical Devices

Born in 1920
His patents by '82 were plenty.

Electronic control systems was his expertise.
His inventions were used with ease.

His work made modern innovations
Possible for various applications.

A control unit for the pacemaker (the heart);
Television and radio resistors (to help them start);

Film resistors for computers
Our everyday troubleshooters;

A burglar proof cash register;
A guided missile variable resistor;

And a chemical filter for air
To avoid breathing despair.

Boykin's impact on our lives
Deserves a place in our nation's archives.

Sources

Aaseng, Nathan. *Black Inventors*. (Facts on File, Inc., 1997), p. xiv.

Gibbs, C. R. *Black Inventors from Africa to America*. (Silver Spring, Maryland: Three Dimensional Publishing Company, 1999), p. 133.

Sammons, Vivian Ovelton. *Blacks in Science and Medicine*. (New York: Hemisphere Publishing Corporation, 1990), p. 34.

U.S. Government Department of Energy Office of Public Affairs. "Black Contribution in Science and Energy Technology". 1979, p. 13.

U.S. Patent Office Microfilm. *Otis Boykin*. Patent No. 3,191,108. June 22, 1965. Great Lakes Patent and Trademark Center. Detroit Public Library. Detroit, Michigan.

U.S. Patent Office Microfilm. *Otis Boykin*. Patent No. 4,461,996. December 31, 1985. December 31, 1982. Great Lakes Patent and Trademark Center. Detroit Public Library. Detroit, Michigan.

U.S. Patent Office Microfilm. *Otis Boykin*. Patent No. 3,394,290. December 31, 1985. July 23, 1968. Great Lakes Patent and Trademark Center. Detroit Public Library. Detroit, Michigan.

Wina Marché

Paul Brown

b. 1917
Invented Multiple Spin Toy (Whizz-zer) 1970
Springfield, Ohio

Engineer, Uncle Paul Brown,
    when his nephew came around,
      tried to spin nephew's top.
He tried and decided to stop.
There must be a better way,
    is what he wanted to say.
The better way took a week
    to experiment, search, and seek.

The result, the *Whizz-zer* spinner
    top, was super and a winner!
After *Whizz-er* he changed careers;
    he left the Corps of Army Engineers.
But first, would you believe
    it took fourteen "nos" to receive
    one "yes" that changed his life.
The rest is history for Paul and wife.

Guess the other companies' vision
    was limited or corporate indecision

made them reject Brown's new idea.

You see Brown didn't shed a tear.

He just knocked on Mattel's door.

A closed door means **try more**!

Brown was sixty times a patentee;

you know giving up wasn't his cup a tea!

Sources

Brodie, James Michael. *Created Equal: The Lives and Ideas of Black American Innovators*. (New York: William Morrow and Company, Inc., 1993), p. 172.

Ebony. October 1998, p. 160.

U.S. Microfilm. *Paul Brown*. No. 3,523,386. August 11, 1970. Great Lakes Patent and Trademark Center. Detroit Public Library. Detroit.

Wina Marché

Dr. George E. Carruthers

b. 1939 - Cincinnati, Ohio
PhD in Aeronautical Engineering
Astrophysicist;
Invented a Lunar Surface Ultraviolet Camera/Spectrograph

George Carruthers
    worked with others
    on Apollo 16,
    exploring the lunar scene.
His 1969 Lunar Surface Ultraviolet
    Camera/Spectrograph
    can make a lunar photograph.
Born in '39 in Cincinnati
    NASA was in his destiny.

His 1972 design
    was also fine.
His cameras capture light
    not seen by human sight.
We can read the lunar atmosphere
    throughout the year
    and study the moon's condition;
    thanks to the Apollo mission.

Sources

Henderson, Susan K. *African American Inventors II* (Mantako, MN: Capstone Press, 1998), p. 17-21.

Sammons, Vivian Ovelton. *Blacks in Science and Medicine.* (New York: Hemisphere Publishing Corporation, 1990), p. 49.

Sullivan, Otha Richard. Haskins, Jim, general editor. *African American Inventors.* (New York: John Wiley & Sons, Inc., 1998), p. 137-142.

U.S. Patent Office Microfilm. *George E. Carruthers.* No. 3,478,216. November 11, 1969. Great Lakes Patent and Trademark Center. Detroit Public Library. Detroit.

Wina Marché

Emmett W. Chappelle

Phoenix, Arizona 1925
Biochemists; Photobiology; Astrochemist;
Light Detection Invention

1925, the year of his birth
    in Arizona, City of Phoenix
    began his journey here on earth,
    a diverse, career, and academic mix,
    gave Chappelle a dual reach
    with research and mission to teach.

All things large, all things small,
    people, animals, plants, microbes,
    things that walk, things that crawl
    are subject to scientific probes
    in search of unknown facts
    about certain habits and impacts

Chappelle had the researcher's bent
    to know what things meant;
    to not know the word can't;
    to know things some so scant;
    some too small for the naked eye;
    some in water, some in the sky.

Chappelle's methods for rapid pace

assessment of bacteria in H_2O

and his scope of outer space

added to what we already know

about things good and adverse;

about organisms and the universe.

Sources

American Men and Woman of Science: The Physical and Biological Sciences. (New York: Bowker, 1970-1983), p. 145.

Ebony, Chicago: Johnson Publishing Co., Nov. 1961, p. 7.

Gibbs, C.R. *Black Inventors from Africa to America.* (Silver Spring, Maryland: Three Dimensional Publishing Company, 1999), p. 122.

U.S. Patent Office Microfilm. *Emmett W. Chappelle.* No. 3,520,660. July 14, 1970. Great Lakes Patent and Trademark Center, Detroit Public Library. Detroit.

U.S. Patent Office Microfilm. *Emmett W. Chappelle.* No. 3,971,703. July 27, 1976. Great Lakes Patent and Trademark Center, Detroit Public Library. Detroit.

U.S. Patent Office Microfilm. *Emmett W. Chappelle*. No. 4,385,223. May 24, 1983. Great Lakes Patent and Trademark Center, Detroit Public Library. Detroit.

Dr. Frank Alphonso Crossley

1925; Chicago, Illinois
PhD 1950 Illinois Institute of Technology
 Metallurgical Engineer;
Seven Patents; Metallurgy Expert

Metallurgy, chemistry, Crossley,
 put them together and you have a patentee.
The seven times patentee brought
 forth ideas aircraft missile folk sought
 about mixed metals' characteristics
 and possible use for submarine ballistics.
Dr. Frank Alphonso Crossley,
 an expert in titanium science technology.

Sources

Sammons, Vivian Ovelton. *Blacks in Science and Medicine*. (New York: Hemisphere Publishing Corporation, 1990), p. 64.

U.S. Patent Office Microfilm. *Frank Alphonso Crossley*. No. 3,117,001. January 7, 1964. Great Lakes Patent and Trademark Center. Detroit Public Library. Detroit.

U.S. Patent Office Microfilm. *Frank Alphonso Crossley*. No. 2,798,807. July 9, 1957. Great Lakes Patent and Trademark Center. Detroit Public Library. Detroit.

U.S. Patent Office Microfilm. *Frank Alphonso Crossley*. No. 4,420,460. December 13, 1983. Great Lakes Patent and Trademark Center. Detroit Public Library. Detroit.

David Nelson Crosthwait, Jr.

(1898-1976) Nashville, Tennessee
Electrical Engineer, Mechanical Engineer
Inventions in Air, Heating, Ventilation

David Crosthwait
until his death in 1976 was a mechanical engineer
who enjoyed a worldwide productive career.
His hands and skill made many contributions
to air, heat, and refrigeration solutions.

The New York Rockefeller Center Complex,
you might say, is his engineering apex.
The control systems for ventilation
and heating are Crosthwait's inspiration.

Many countries the world over agree
that Crosthwait was an ingenious patentee.
His patents total 114,
and many more ideas he had overseen.

Sources

Gibbs, C.R. *Black Inventors from Africa to America.* (Silver Spring, Maryland: Three Dimensional Publishing Company, 1999), p. 121.

Sullivan, Otha Richard. Haskins, Jim, general editor. *African American Inventors.* (New York: John Wiley & Sons, Inc., 1998), p. 89-92.

U. S. Patent Office Microfilm. *David Nelson Crosthwait, Jr.* Patent No. 1,353,457. September 23, 1920. Great Lakes Patent and Trademark Center. Detroit Public Library. Detroit.

U. S. Patent Office Microfilm. *David Nelson Crosthwait, Jr.* Patent No. 1,661,323. March 6, 1928. Great Lakes Patent and Trademark Center. Detroit Public Library. Detroit.

U. S. Patent Office Microfilm. *David Nelson Crosthwait, Jr.* Patent No. 1,755,430. April 22, 1930. Great Lakes Patent and Trademark Center. Detroit Public Library. Detroit.

Dr. A. W. Curtis

1911; West Virginia- Cornell University
Dr. George Washington Carver's Assistant
Detroit Inventor-Researcher-Manufacturer

Suppose your life had an historical day
    especially if you became a protégé.
Dr. Curtis had this experience one year
    after graduation and as he began his career.
A fellowship is how they met.
    How lucky can a young graduate get?

As Dr. Carver's protégé he helped seek
    answers about products and get unique
results from ordinary things we eat;
    like fruits, vegetables and sweet
potatoes and other foods of everyday.
    Seeking to use them in a different way.

Dr. Curtis started a foundation
    for Dr. Carver as a legacy for the nation.
Detroit is where he decided to settle
    planting his roots and testing his mettle.
He opened A. W. Curtis Laboratories
    and invented health inventories.

Sources

Detroit Area Pre-College Engineering Program (DAPCEP). Minority
   Contributors. Detroit: DAPCEP, 1991, p. 127.

"Experimental Energy". Michigan Chronicle. February 16-22, 2000.
   p. 1c.

http://travel.michigan.org/detail/.asp?m=28p.=B

http://www.detroit.accommodationscenter.com/a

Dr. Lincoln I. Diuguid

b. 1917 Lynchburg, Virginia
PhD Organic Chemistry 1945 Cornell University
Invented Burning Efficiency Enhancement Method

Dr. Lincoln I. Diuguid (Do-Good)
  found in 1947 folk would
  hire him if he denied being Black;
  or they'd put his workplace in the back.

With his impressive honor credentials
  and imbued with Cornell potential;
  plus two years post grad hours;
  reasons to be hired with fanfare and flowers!

Undaunted by the ever present race card
  Dr. Diuguid chose to work very hard
  at teaching others how to excel.
  He did. His students did very well.

After thirty-three years in 1982
  he didn't really say "adieu"
  to chemistry. His Company, Diuguid,
  manufactured and produced everything it could!

Wina Marché

From his laboratory and mind
    came products of every kind;
    for home, for body, the face.
Carefully produced at his own pace.

Though 1947 folk with hiring power weren't nice
    Dr. Lincoln I. Diuguid took his own advice.
    With his talent, dignity, and self worth
    made a difference in lives on planet earth!

Sources

McKissack, Patricia and McKissack, Frederick. *African Americans Inventors*. (Brookfield, Connecticut: The Millbrook Press, 1994), p. 86-88.

Phelps, Shirelle and Matney, Jr., William C. editors. *Who's Who Among Black Americans*. (Detroit: Gale Research Inc., 1994), p. 396.

U. S. Patent Microfilm. *Lincoln Isaiah Diuguid*. No. 4,539,015. September 3, 1985. Great Lakes Patent and Trademark Center. Detroit Public Library. Detroit, Michigan.

Who's Who Among Black Americans. (Northbrook, Illinois: Who's Who Among Black Americans Publishing Co., 1985), p. 227.

Clarence L. Elder

Born 1935; Attended Morgan State College

Invented an Occustat in 1976; Patented in Baltimore, Maryland

Elder invented an occustat

It is for business or public habitat.

This electronic machinery

Saves thirty percent energy.

The occustat's electronic beam

Works with the temperature as a team.

The beam raises or lowers the temperature;

Consistent hot and cold it can ensure.

Elder is an inventor international.

He and his staff have the wherewithal

For twelve trademarks, patents, and copyrights

In the U.S. as well as in foreign sites.

Sources

U.S. Government. *Black Contributions in Science and Energy Technology.* (A Pamphlet Containing Biographical Sketches of 24

Black Inventors Who Made Contributions in Science and Energy Technology, no date), p. 20-21.

U.S. Patent Office Microfilm. *Clarence L. Elder*. No. 3,556,531. January 19, 1971. Great Lakes Patent and Trademark Center. Detroit Public Library. Detroit.

U.S. Patent Office Microfilm. *Clarence L. Elder*. No. 3,165,188. January 12, 1965. Great Lakes Patent and Trademark Center. Detroit Public Library. Detroit.

U.S. Patent Office Microfilm. *Clarence L. Elder*. No, 4,000,400. December 28, 1976. Great Lakes Patent and Trademark Center. Detroit Public Library. Detroit.

Dr. Meredith C. Gourdine

b. 1929 - Livingston, New Jersey;

PhD Engineering 1960 California Institute of Technology

Invented an Incineraid; Electricity from Gas;

Technique to Disperse Airport Fog; Over 70 Patents

Meredith Gourdine's incineraid

was paid

much attention.

His invention

was for reduction

of garbage smoke production

in dwellings like apartments.

It was licensed by city governments

before their new disposal plan

that imposed a garbage burning ban.

He and his company team

invented on their own steam.

They have patents in gas dynamics

and specialize in electronics.

Gourdine's '87 expertise in fogs

eased airport runaway traffic clogs.

His painting machine for the assembly line

painted hard to reach surfaces just fine.

Meredith Gourdine, an electrical engineering PhD, is a National Academy of Engineering inductee.

Sources

Aaseng, Nathan. *Black Inventors*. (New York: Facts On File, 1997), p. xiv.

Gibbs, C. R. *Black Inventors: From Africa to America*. (*Silver Spring, Maryland:* Three Dimensional Publishing Company, 1995), p. 122, 147.

Henderson, Susan K. *African American Inventors, II*. (Mankato, MN: Capstone Press, 1998), p. 23-29.

Sullivan, Richard Otha. Haskins, Jim, general editor. *African American Inventors*. (New York: John Wiley & Sons, Inc., 1998), p. 120-122.

U.S. Patent Microfilm. *Meredith C. Gourdine*. No. 3,582,694. June 1, 1971. Great Lakes Patent and Trademark Center. Detroit Public Library. Detroit, Michigan.

U.S. Patent Microfilm. *Meredith C. Gourdine*. No. 4,574,092. March 4, 1986. Great Lakes Patent and Trademark Center. Detroit Public Library. Detroit, Michigan.

U.S. Patent Microfilm. *Meredith C. Gourdine*. No. 4,671,805. June 9, 1987. Great Lakes Patent and Trademark Center. Detroit Public Library. Detroit, Michigan.

Other Patents 1990-1996

   4,916,033   5,297,005   5,422,787   5,456,596   5,487,957
5,548,907

Van Sertima, Ivan, editor. *Blacks in Science: Ancient and Modern.* (New Brunswick: Transaction Books, 1992), p. 226-227.

Bessie Blount Griffin

Physical Therapist (1914) Hickory, Virginia
Inventions – Portable Receptacle Supports

Bessie Griffin, a physical therapist,
    worked with WWII amputees.
She had several ideas on her list
    of patient problems she could ease.
One – the ability to self feed
    was a patient's great need.

Patients sitting or prone
    could handle Bessie's device
    and manage feeding on their own.
Bessie invented such an aid twice.
    When there was no marketing chance,
    she signed her patents over to France.

Sources

Bessie Blount (Griffin) *http://www.inventorsmuseum.com/Bessie* Blount.html.
http://inventors.about.com

U.S. Patent Office Microfilm. *Bessie Griffin*. No. 2,550,554. April 24, 1951. Great Lakes Patent and Trademark Center. Detroit Public Library. Detroit, Michigan.

Wina Marché

Claude Harvard

Highland Park, MI (1911-1999)
Inventor 29 Patents

This story begins
    with several spins,
    first a crystal radio,
    then the desire to know
    what makes it play;
    inside where secrets stay.

A school of trade
    became Harvard's crusade.
    Despite enrollment objections
    Claude made the school connections.
    He graduated at the top,
    but faced the red light STOP!

No promised journeyman's card.
    Not to be bitter was hard.
    Then he was twenty-three.
    Perhaps there was another key;
    another road, another door.
    Perhaps there would be an encore.

Then came Henry Ford's attention
    due to Claude's invention,
    a piston testing machine,
    whose like had not been seen.
    It was his idea, one,
    twenty-eight more were to come!

Yes, there was an encore.
    Someone settled the score
    with a journeyman's card.
    Despite previous disregard,
    Harvard received it, though late,
    after a sixty-five year wait!

Some many years from today
    those who caused the card delay
    will remain in oblivion – obscurity,
    blotted from the pages of history.
    But Harvard's name, inventions, deeds, and plight
    are the matters about which historians write!

Harvard was a gracious man
    throughout his life span.
    Admired for his skill
    his indomitable will;
    his inspiring and caring;
    his teaching and sharing.

299

Sources

DeRamus, Betty. 'It's the ones we don't hear about who are the greats'. *Detroit Free Press*, August 18, 1999.

Elrick, M. L. Obituary: *Claude Harvard: Inventor surpassed discrimination*. Detroit *Free Press*, July 2, 1999.

Allen-Williams, Cheryl, editor. *Pathfinders: Afro-American Achievers and Inventors*. (Detroit: Michigan Consolidated Gas Company, no date).

James E. Huntley

Washington, D.C.

Inventor of an Emergency Fire Escape

Huntley back in 1975
    was thinking of ways to survive.
His emergency fire device
    was portable and did suffice
    at home, work or play
    when a fire blocked the way.

Source

U.S. Patent Office Microfilm. *James E. Huntley*. No. 3,880,255. April 29, 1975. U.S. Patent & Trademark Center. Detroit Public Library. Detroit, Michigan.

Wina Marché

Harry and Mary E. Jackson

Protective Appliances for the Home
April 21, 1936- Harrisburg, PA.
by Wina Marché

Days of old-
    many stories
    do unfold
    about the glories
    folk did behold.

Doors unlocked
    they felt good
    windows unblocked;
    the neighborhood
    was united
    against the uninvited.

Now they lock the door,
    set the alarm
    for the home and more.
    The Jacksons knew
    the customs they outgrew.

Their inventions, three,

    are safety appliances

    that oversee

    other alliances

    watching the domicile

    in the meanwhile.

Sources

U.S. Patent Office Microfilm. *Harry and Mary Jackson.* 2,038,491. April 21, 1936. Great Lakes Patent and Trademark Center. Detroit Public Library. Detroit, Michigan.

U.S. Patent Office Microfilm. *Harry and Mary Jackson.* 2,053,035. September 1, 1936. Great Lakes Patent and Trademark Center. Detroit Public Library. Detroit, Michigan.

U.S. Patent Office Microfilm. *Harry and Mary Jackson.* 2,071,343. February 23, 1937. Great Lakes Patent and Trademark Center. Detroit Public Library. Detroit, Michigan.

Wina Marché

Richard H. Jackson

1933 Detroit, Michigan

Engineer – Designed Parts for Commercial Aircraft

Richard H. Jackson, engineer
    is no stranger to aircraft gear.
Boeing 747 landing gear system
    was designed by him.
His thrust reverser fail-safe, too
    was designed with Boeing purview.

Beech Aircraft, NASA got his advice
    when they needed info precise.
The U. S. Department of Defense
    used Jackson's engineering sense
    for Gemini Space flights V through
    XII along with research by the crew.

Sources

"Experimental History". *Michigan Chronicle*. Detroit. February 16-22, 2002, p. c2.

Sammons, Vivian Ovelton. *Blacks in Science and Medicine*. (New York: Hemisphere Publishing Corporation, 1990), p. 129.

Dr. James A. Parsons, Jr.

1900s
Chief Chemist/Metallurgist at
Age 27 for Duriron Co. of Dayton, Ohio;
Electrochemist; Metallurgist
Inventor-Corrison Resisting Ferrous Alloy

Dr. James Parsons, Jr.,
> many times a patentee,
> earned a Rensselaer
> Polytechnic Institute degree.

His corrison resisting
> ideas were heeded
> by industry for
> they were much needed.

Sources

Carwell, Hattie. *Blacks in Science: Astrophysicist to Zoologist.* (Hicksville, New York: Exposition Press, 1977), p. 45.

Gibbs, C. R. *Black Inventors from Africa to America.* (Silver Springs, Maryland: Three Dimensional Publishing Company, 1999), p. 114, 119.

McKissack, Patricia and McKissack, Frederick. *African American Inventors.* (Brookfield, Connecticut Millbrook Pres, 1994), p. 90.

U.S. Patent Office Microfilm. *James A. Parsons, Jr.* No. 1,728,360. September 17, 1929. Great Lakes Patent and Trademark Center. Detroit Public Library. Detroit.

U.S. Patent Office Microfilm. *James A. Parsons, Jr.* No. 1,972,103. September 4, 1934. Great Lakes Patent and Trademark Center. Detroit Public Library. Detroit.

Victor L. Ransom

New Shrewsbury, New Jersey
Inventor – A Traffic Data System

Driving can please you
    more than walking or the tram.
Driving can steal your leisure
    in a traffic jam.
You would rather a running trot
    than drive in a moving parking lot!

Victor Ransom's data gathering process
    could ease your driving stress.
His system collects the info
    so in advance you'll know
    when traffic is
    stop and go!

Sources

U.S. Patent Office Microfilm. *Victor L. Ransom*. 3,231,866. January 25, 1966. Great Lakes Patent and Trademark Center. Detroit Public Library. Detroit, Michigan.

U.S. Patent Office Microfilm. *Victor L. Ransom.* 3,866,185. February 11, 1975. Great Lakes Patent and Trademark Center. Detroit Public Library. Detroit, Michigan.

Mary Jane Reynolds

Invention: Hoisting and Lifting Mechanism- 1920
Patent Registered in St. Joseph, Missouri

A hoisting and lifting mechanism
    Reynolds did invent
    with the intent
    of saving your back
    from an ache attack.
Her device did the work
    without a quirk
    or muscle jerk.

Source

U.S. Patent Microfilm. *Mary Jane Reynolds*. No. 1,337,667. April 20, 1920. Great Lakes Patent and Trademark Center. Detroit Public Library. Detroit, Michigan.

Frank B. Sewell

1919

Inventor- Entrepreneur- Painex Pain Reliever

Detroit, Michigan

Frank Sewell started out
    as sales manager for
    A.W. Curtis Company.
Later he started
    his own company- Painex.
His clients grew and were devout.

They praise and recommend
    Ringmaster Rubbing Oil.
For fifty years folk
    have experienced relief
    from assorted aches
    using Ringmaster's special blend.

Source

Michigan Chronicle. "Ringmaster Rubbing Oil Makes 50- Year
    Milestone. July 25-29, 2000. p. 1A, 4A, Detroit, Michigan.

Dr. Robert Shurney

b. 1900-Physicist;
Aerospace Engineer; Tennessee State University
Inventor – Moon Buggy Tires for 1972 Apollo 15
*   Space Food Utensils*

Many folk would
    like to go
    to the moon,
    anytime soon.

Shurney didn't go but sent
    the wire mesh tires
    that he helped invent
    for the moon buggy
    in the Apollo 15
    moon exploring scene.

Sources

Aaseng, Nathan. *Black Inventors*. (New York: Facts on File, 1997),
    p. xv.

Burns, Khephra, and Miles, William. *Black Stars in Orbit: NASA's African American Astronauts*. (San Diego: Gulliver Books-Harcourt Brace & Company, 1995), p. 30, 31.

Ebony. "Dupont Presents 110 Years of Blacks in Science". Chicago: Johnson Publishing Co., December, 1999, p. 85-91.

Sullivan, Otha Richard. *African American Inventors*. (New York: John Wiley & Sons, Inc., 1998), p. 142.

Van Sertima, Ivan, editor. *Blacks in Science: Ancient and Modern*. (New Brunswick: Transaction Books, 1992), p. 190.

Jake Simmons, Jr.

Invention – a Windshield Wiper;
Entrepreneur; Petroleum Millionaire
Muskogee County, Oklahoma (1901-1981)

By 1901, Jake's birth year,
    family strife was not a fear.
His ancestors had truly paid the price.
Grandfather, "Cow Tom", made the sacrifice
    from slavery to Black tribal chief
enabling Jake's pride and self-belief.

Childhood probably had many delights
    from his African and Creek birth rights.
He could ride horses very well by age ten.
Later he trained racing horses to win.
Jake deserves the fancy horse rider name-
    equestrian, which, of course, means the same.

Jake left the ranch to be educated
    at Tuskegee, the best and "high rated".
He was enjoying his learning life.
So much so that he got a wife.
Detroit City became their new home;
    work was the factory and auto chrome.

He liked being his own boss
    which was the corporate world's loss.
Jake invented a useful device
    to free windshields of frost and ice.
His superiors ignored his invention,
    in fact, it got very little mention.

Meanwhile, back at his father's ranch
    some one needed to wave an olive branch.
Perhaps, Jake's father was "raging mad"
    and used all the power he had
    to force Jake to return to Muskogee
Jake surrendered to his father's decree.

Perhaps, experiencing a closed door
    is what helped Jake to soar.
And soar he did to another height,
    with oil deals he was able to expedite
    for Blacks, Native Americans, and Whites.
He got fair prices and protected birth rights.

Jake also became a millionaire
    helping African nations get their share
    of profits from the international oil yield.
Jake's expertise leveled the "playing field".

He especially aided Ghana's progress

    in attaining oil industry success.

It was in the year 1978

    that they did gratitude state

    with the country's Grand Medal Award

    making Jake's good deeds a matter of record.

True, inventor Jake faced a closed door,

    but he became an international

    door opener and more!

Sources

Greenberg, Jonathan. **Staking a Claim**: *Jake Simmons, Jr., and the Making of An African American Oil Dynasty*. (New York: Dutton/Plume, 1991.

Haskins, Jim. *Black Stars: African American Entrepreneurs*. (New York: John Wiley & Sons, Inc., 1998), p. 97-100.

Wina Marché

Homer Smith

1900-1989

Detroit

Inventor - 13 Patents – Entrepreneur

As an inventor Homer Smith
    not only had success with
thirteen U.S. patents
    but they had many intents.

The nineteen fifty-one invention,
    bottle disposal was the intention.
Smith's invention was a bottle breaker –
    those not wanted by the deposit taker.

Homer Smith, the creative workman,
    invented a machine that could crush a can.
He was quite a entrepreneur, too
    with business enterprises, quite a few.

Sources

Gavrilovich, Peter and McGraw, Bill. eds. *The Detroit Almanac: 300 Years of Life in the Motor City.* (Detroit: Detroit Free Press, 2001), p. 192.

National Inventors Hall of Fame. www.invent.org

Richard B. Spikes

Invented An Automatic Car Wash; Auto Directional Signals;
An Automatic Gear
Shift; transmission and Shifting Thereof; Brake System Combining
Hydraulic and Electrical Apparatus
(d. 1963)

Richard B. Spikes, auto
    inventor supreme,
    lived not so long ago
    and was held in high esteem.

His ideas had an impact
    on gears and turn signals, to be exact.
    Spike's automotive inventions
    also included transmissions.

Spikes patented an automatic car wash, too
    which made auto washing easier to do.
    By his death in 1963
    he was also a hydraulic brake patentee.

Sources

Burt, McKinley, Jr. *Black Inventors of America.* (Portland, Oregon: National Book Co., 1969), p. 44-51.

U.S. Patent Office Microfilm. *Richard B. Spikes.* No. 1,889,814. December 6, 1932. Great Lakes Patent and Trademark Center. Detroit Public Library. Detroit, Michigan.

U.S. Patent Office Microfilm. *Richard B. Spikes.* No. 1,936,966. November 28, 1933. Great Lakes Patent and Trademark Center. Detroit Public Library. Detroit, Michigan.

U.S. Patent Office Microfilm. *Richard B. Spikes.* No. 3,015,522. January 2, 1962. Great Lakes Patent and Trademark Center. Detroit Public Library. Detroit, Michigan.

Wina Marché

Rufus Stokes

Invention: Clean Air Machine
Chicago; (1924-1986)

About modern technology
    we complain.
We enjoy the gain
    but not the pain.

Often modern invention
    we enjoy with pride
    but forget to mention
    there is often a down side.

If your eyes and nose burn
    from breathing air pollution,
    and you have a concern
    Rufus Stokes had a solution.

His device reduces gas
    and furnace ash emission.
Any test his device can pass
    whatever the composition.

Rufus didn't finish high school;

He found folk wanted certification

proof, first, as a general rule

before financing natural application.

Sources

Detroit Public Library, Main Branch.

Rufus Stokes. News Files. History and Travel.

http://www.princeton.edu/~mcbrown/displaystokes.html

Ross, T. Roosevelt. *Inventor Has Patent, Needs Financing*. Detroit: Michigan Chronicle, 1981.

U.S. Patent Office Microfilm. *Rufus Stokes*. No. 3,378,241. April 16, 1968. Great Lakes Patent and Trademark Center. Detroit Public Library. Detroit, Michigan.

U.S. Patent Microfilm. *Rufus Stokes*. No. 3,520,113. July 14, 1970. Great Lakes Patent and Trademark Center. Detroit Public Library. Detroit, Michigan.

Wina Marché

Rufus Weaver

Patent Registered in New London, CT. (1900s)
Invention: A Stair Climbing Wheelchair

Rufus Weaver
    was an achiever.
    He invented
    a wheelchair
    that   stair.
    could   a
          climb

Sources

Jet, Chicago: Johnson Publishing Co., May 1, 1969, p. 51.

U.S. Patents by African Americans. An African American Bibliography: Science, Medicine, and Allied Fields: Selected Sources from the Collections of the New York State Library, 1991, p. 14.

U.S. Patent Office Microfilm. *Rufus Weaver*. No. 3,411,598. November 19, 1968. Great Lakes Patent and Trademark Center. Detroit Public Library. Detroit, Michigan.

Ferdinand D. Wharton

St. Louis, Missouri

Invention- Use of Polyelectrolytes for Intestinal Pain- 1972

Wharton's invention in '72,

    was a solution for what to do

    when the intestines are attacked

    and you're feeling sorta whacked.

It involved basic polyelectrolyte

    polymers with certain might.

    Designed to ease that inner pain,

    discomfort and physical strain.

Source

U.S. Patent Office Microfilm. *Ferdinand D. Wharton*. No. 4,655,869. April 11, 1972. U.S. Patent and Trademark Center. Detroit Public Library. Detroit, Michigan.

Wina Marché

Dr. O.S. "Ozzie" Williams

Aeronautical Engineer, (1921); University of New York
Vice President Grunman International-West Africa
Invention: First Airborne Radar Beacon to Locate Lost Aircraft

"Ozzie" Williams, aeronautical engineer,
 inventor, understood aircraft gear.
When an aircraft loses its way
 his airborne radar beacon saves the day.
Lunar lander's guidance rocket
 engines, too, were on his work docket.
Ozzie's aeronautical inventing
 was supporting and preventing.

Sources

Brodie, James Michael. *Created Equal: The Lives and Ideas of Black Innovators*. (New York: William Morrow and Company, Inc., 1993), p. 174-175.

Ebony. September, 1970. Chicago: Johnson Publishing Co., p. 36.

U.S. Government Department of Energy Office of Public Affairs. "Black Contributors to Science and Energy Technology", 1979, p. 12-13.

PART TWELVE

MODERN INVENTORS

Mohammed Bah Abba

From the Homeland, Nigeria
Teacher, Descendant of Potmakers
Invented "Pot in Pot Preservation Cooling System"
$75,000 Winner of Rolex Award for Enterprise

Rolex's Award for Enterprise
    is for ideas creative and wise.
Abba's idea many people enable
    by preserving food for their table.

In a rural Nigerian town
    food once turned black and brown,
    spoilage, no refrigeration.
Now there's cause for celebration.
A Nigerian teacher's solution
    works without ozone pollution
    with water, clay pots, and sand;
    ingredients he had on hand.

"Pot in Pot Cooling System", the name
    that brought Abba fortune and fame.
A small food filled pot of clay,
    to keep unwanted heat away,
    is placed in a wet sand filled pot;

327

a wet, cloth cover cools the lot.

"Cooling pots" many folk can afford.

because of Abba's $75,000 award

Sources

http://www.time.com/time/2001/inventions/basi

rolexawards.com

Time. "A New Way to Keep Food Cool!". November 19, 2001, p. 90.

Christopher P. Adams

Boston; Patent Issued 1997
Invention; Uses of Nucleic Acid

Christopher Adams understood
    biochemistry and what would
    be a good combination
    in a chemical relation
    for some foods and nucleic acid
    for your digestion to be placid.

Source

U.S. Patent Office Microfilm. *Christopher P. Adams*. No. 5,641,658. June 24, 1997. U.S. Patent and Trademark Center. Detroit Public Library. Detroit, Michigan.

Dr. George E. Alcorn

Born 1942; B.A. Physics; M.S. Nuclear Physics;
PhD Atomic and Molecular Physics;
1994 Honored by Howard University as a Black Achiever;
Invented an Imaging X-Ray Spectrometer

Dr. George E. Alcorn
   has twelve plus eight
      inventions that indicate
         to semiconductors he can relate.
            He worked in missile defense
               and planetary intelligence.
                  His knowledge about these things is immense.

Dr. George E. Alcorn
   was 1984 Inventor of the Year.
      That year was a high in his NASA career.
         1984 was again a banner year.
            He received a medal that was dear
               honoring his work as NASA-EEO
                  helping minority recruitment grow.

Dr. George E. Alcorn
   by sharing his time and gift
      manages to give others a lift.

He founded the Saturday Academy.

It helps to increase inner-city youths'

ability in math and science so they can choose

science careers and offer them info to peruse.

Sources

Brown, Mitchell C. *Faces of African Americans in the Sciences. url:http://www.Princeton.edu/~mcbrowndisplay/faces.html (update 2-16-2002).*

George Edward Alcorn-Physicist of the African Diaspora. http://www.math.buffalo.edu/mad/physics/alcor

George Edward Alcorn, Jr. Physicist, Inventor. http://www.Princeton.edu/~brown/display/alc

U.S. Patent Office Microfilm. *George E. Alcorn.* No. 4,618,380. October 21, 1986. U.S. Patent and Trademark Center. Detroit Public Library. Detroit.

U.S. Patent Office Microfilm. *George E. Alcorn.* No. 4,543,422. September 24, 1985. U.S. Patent and Trademark Center. Detroit Public Library. Detroit.

U.S. Patent Office Microfilm. *George E. Alcorn.* No. 4,727,282. September 18, 1984. U.S. Patent and Trademark Center. Detroit Public Library. Detroit.

U.S. Patent Office Microfilm. *George E. Alcorn*. No. 4,289,834. September 15, 1981. U.S. Patent and Trademark Center. Detroit Public Library. Detroit.

Williams, Dr. Scott. Professor of Mathematics University of New York at Buffalo. "George Edward Alcorn-Physicist of the African Diaspora", p. 1-3. http://www.math.buffalo.edu/mad/special/index

Chris Allen

Entrepreneur – Owner of Arthur's Place (2000 Artho Aquatic Fitness Center)

Tom Ballard – Engineer- Designer

Chris Allen certainly had no idea
    he'd start a new business career.
It began with his wife's need for
    him to do a good deed.
He ran a tub of warm water to aid
    the easing of aches nine holes of golf made!
Indeed, the warm water eased her pain;
    no aches; she was feeling fine again!

Allen knew the well established fact
    that warm water has a positive impact.
He contacted a friend with the idea,
    Tom Ballard, an inventor engineer.
Ballard listened and captured the gist,
    and became the designer and artist.
He drew an exercise concept
    that a pain therapist might accept.

The result- Artho Aquatic Fitness
    System Allen's soothing process.

The praise for Arthur's Place

 is in a customer's smiling face.

It is sheer happiness folk feel

 when relief from misery is real.

Arthur's Place, Allen's health center,

 chases pain yearly summer to winter.

Sources

Anstett, Patricia. "Easing the Pain". *Detroit Free Press*. May 9, 2000,
 p. 10F-12F.

*http://www.credopub.com/archives/2001/iss20010507/20010507p09.h
tm*

http://www.fitnessmanagement.com/info/inro-pa

Tanya Allen

Inventor- Disposable Undergarments (Ever Fresh)
Detroit, 1994

Tanya Allen addressed a need.
  Folk saw the need and agreed.
    Her disposable undergarment
      Had a special, initial intent.
        Now with diverse clients and use
          Allen is able to mass produce.

Sources

Ebony. October 1998, p. 159.

U.S. Patent Office Microfilm. *Tanya Allen*. No. 5,325,543. July 5, 1994. U.S. Patent & Trademark Center. Detroit Public Library. Detroit, Michigan.

Sharon Janel Barnes

Beaumont, Texas – (b 1955); Lake Jackson, Texas; Chemist
Inventor (Team of Five) Contactless Measurement of
Sample Temperature

The girl who was young
  eager to learn and gifted
didn't know that her parents'
  family philosophy had lifted
her to a frame of mind that was
  success-bound and productive.
The family philosophy was
  positive and constructive.

Versatile, spiritually balanced,
  gifted, respected, and Black.
Sharon is a lady for all seasons.
  She is giving the community back
her gift, her enthusiasm, her time.
  This active, many times awardee
is a volunteer, city council member;
  a leader, and a governor appointee.

As wife, mother, church, volunteer;
  she is good at the time balancing act.

She has been Mayor Pro Tem; a state

    commissioner as a matter of fact.

The community knows her as

    the ultimate gifted, giving, achiever.

Her theater activities prove that she

    is a "value the arts" believer.

Sharon Janel Barnes' productive

    sojourn here is no surprise.

Father and Mother went to college;

    their children were to do likewise.

Sharon's career path – high school,

    Bachelor of Science degree;

Dow Chemical Company chemist;

    lead to the title chemical patentee.

Sources

E-mail Biographical Information *Sharon Janel Barnes* 3-19-02.

Sullivan, Otha Richard. *Black Stars: African American Women Scientists & Inventors*. General editor. Jim Haskins. (New York: John Wiley & Sons, Inc., 2002, p. 108-111.

U.S. Patent Microfilm. *Sharon J. Barnes, et al.* No. 4,988,211. January 29, 1991. U.S. Patent & Trademark Center. Detroit Public Library.

Dr. Patricia E. Bath

b. 1943 - Los Angeles

Invented; Cataract Laserphaco Probe; Ophthalmologist

Her invention uses

    laser power to

    vaporize cataracts

    from patients' eyes.

The invention is

    quick, painless,

    a welcomed improvement.

Another invention

    helped restore eyesight.

Dr. Bath developed her

    skills at several

    institutions of higher learning.

Howard Medical School

    in nineteen sixty-eight –

    advanced study at

    New York U. and Columbia U.

Her "firsts" include

    becoming a surgeon

At UCLA Medical

Center-the first
lady faculty
at UCLA Jules
Stein Eye Institute.

Sources

"DuPont Presents 110 Years of Blacks in Science". *Ebony*. Chicago: Johnson Publishing Co., December, 1999. p. 85-91.

Henderson, Susan K. *African American Inventors, III*. (Mankato, MN: Capstone Press, 1998), p. 9-13.

Sullivan, Otha Richard, Haskins, Jim, general editor. *Black Stars: African American Women Scientists & Inventors*. (New York: John Wiley & Son, Inc., 2002.), p. 88-91.

U.S. Patent Office Microfilm. *Patricia E. Bath*. No, 4,744,360. May 17, 1988. Patent & Trademark Center. Detroit Public Library. Detroit, Michigan.

U.S. Patent Office Microfilm. *Patricia E. Bath*. No, 5,843,971. December 1, 1998. U.S. Patent & Trademark Center. Detroit Public Library. Detroit, Michigan.

U.S. Patent Office Microfilm. *Patricia E. Bath*. No, 5,919,186. July 6, 1999. U.S. Patent & Trademark Center. Detroit Public Library. Detroit, Michigan.

Billie J. Becoat

b. 1938 - Centralia, Illinois
Invented Two Wheel Drive Bike;
Four Wheel Drive Scootabike

Inventions often come from need
    with Becoat this was the case, indeed!
His son's bike needed repair,
    the chain needed frequent care.
Becoat needed to find a way
    for his repairs to last and stay!

The two wheel drive was the solution,
    Becoat's clever chain contribution
to a safe, controlled, easy ride;
    no slippery surface slip and slide!
It rides well on rough ground and hills
    regardless of the bike rider's skills.

Becoat is a very versatile man;
    a college biology man.;
    a mechanics man;
    a blues and guitar man;
    a home improvement man;
    his son's repair man.
Now he's an inventing man.

Sources

Gibbs, C. R. *Black Inventors from Africa to America*. (Silver Spring, Maryland: Three Dimensional Publishing Company, 1999), p. 126.

Henderson, Susan K. *African American Inventors II*. (Mankato, MN.: Capstone Press, 1998), p. 9-15.

U.S. Patent Office Microfilm. *Billie J. Becoat*. No. 4,895,385. January 23, 1990. Great Lakes Patent and Trademark Center. Detroit Public Library. Detroit, Michigan.

U.S. Patent Office Microfilm. *Billie J. Becoat*. No. 5,004,258. April 2, 1991. Great Lakes Patent and Trademark Center. Detroit Public Library. Detroit, Michigan.

U.S. Patent Office Microfilm. *Billie J. Becoat*. No. 5,116,070. May 25, 1992. Great Lakes Patent and Trademark Center. Detroit Public Library. Detroit, Michigan.

U.S. Patent Office Microfilm. *Billie J. Becoat*. No. 5,184,838. February 9, 1993. Great Lakes Patent and Trademark Center. Detroit Public Library. Detroit, Michigan.

Dr. J. Theodore Brown, Jr.

State University of New York, Stony Brook

Developer of an Over the Counter Drug Test

Dr. Brown's over the
    Counter Drug Test project
Took time, research and
    13 years to perfect.
He achieved one of his
    goals- universal access.
It is a commodity
    everyone can possess.

Dr. Brown urges parents
    to use his test
Early, very early to beat
    the drug dealer's quest.
He suggests that parents
    start educating
Before their children
    start contemplating.

Sources

"Black Man Creates First Over the Counter Home Drug Test Approved by FDA"....*Jet*. February 17, 19978, p. 10-11.

CNN-FDA Approves Over-the-Counter Drug Test

http://www.cnn.com/HEALTH/9701/21/home.drug.t

*http://www.*ndsn.org/FEB97/HOMETEST.html

Dr. Michael E. Croslin

St. Croix, U.S. Virgin Islands; b. 1933
Forest Hills Gardens, New York
BS. Mechanical Engineering; MS. Electrical Engineering:
PhD Biomedical Engineering 1968; New York University
Invention: Computerized Blood Pressure Machine (Medtek 410)

You probably can't even imagine
how life would be as a child
if your parents ran away
and left you while
you were still a baby
and no relatives, no one
came to take you home
and call you their own.

Michael was taken in by
a family on the island.
At age twelve Michael
decided to expand
his boundaries for
a new life in the U.S.;
so he ran away to two states.
Wisconsin offered progress.

345

At age 14 he graduated from
   high school. At seventeen
      he had a college degree;
         an achievement unforeseen
            at such an early age.
               This state was good for him.
                  The future had a new look,
                     bright rather than dim.

Dr. Croslin is over forty times
   A U.S. patentee.
      Trying his hand at business
         He earned another degree.
            This time a Masters in
               Business administration
                  To insure good business
                     and technology correlation.

Sources

Brodie, Michael James. *Created Equal: The Lives and Ideas of Black American Innovators*. (New York: William Morrow Company, Inc., 1993), p. 169-172.

*Http://www.omhrc.gov/inetpub/wwwroot/omhrc/conferences/blkhistor
y.htm* "A Celebration of Black History". 4/17/02.

Sullivan, Otha Richard. Jim Haskins, general editor. *African American Inventors*. (New York: John Wiley & Sons, Inc., 1998), p. 123-126.

U.S. Patent Office Microfilm. *Michael E. Croslin*. No. 4,407,297. October 4, 1983. Great Lakes Patent and Trademark Center. Detroit Public Library. Detroit.

U.S. Patent Office Microfilm. *Michael E. Croslin*. No. 4,338,949. July 13, 1982. Great Lakes Patent and Trademark Center. Detroit Public Library. Detroit.

U.S. Patent Office Microfilm. *Michael E. Croslin*. No. 4,326,537. April 27, 1982. Great Lakes Patent and Trademark Center. Detroit Public Library. Detroit, Michigan.

U.S. Patent Office Microfilm. *Michael E. Croslin*. No. 4,271,844. June 9, 1981. Great Lakes Patent and Trademark Center. Detroit Public Library. Detroit, Michigan.

U.S. Patent Office Microfilm. *Michael E. Croslin*. No. 3,975,960. August 24, 1976. Great Lakes Patent and Trademark Center. Detroit Public Library. Detroit, Michigan.

U.S. Patent Office Microfilm. *Michael E. Croslin*. No. 3,756,292. September 4, 1973. Great Lakes Patent and Trademark Center. Detroit Public Library. Detroit, Michigan.

U.S. Patent Office Microfilm. *Michael E. Croslin*. No. 3,581,734. June 1, 1971. Great Lakes Patent and Trademark Center. Detroit Public Library. Detroit, Michigan.

Dr. Mark Dean

*Electrical Engineer, IBM; Bachelor of Science Electrical
Engineering (BSEE)*

Master of Science Electrical Engineering (MSEE)

A Microcomputer System; Co-Invention with Dennis Moeller

Dr. Mark Dean's vitals –

born March 2,

1957:

Jefferson City, Tennessee

BSEE degree- 1979

University of Tennessee –

MSEE. – 1982

Florida. Atlanta U.

Doctorate – 1992

Stanford U. also in

Electrical Engineering

Dr. Dean has many more titles.

He is a patentee

more than 20 times.

IBM V.P. 1996

IBM Fellow – 1997

Black Engineer of the Year

inductee National

Inventors Hall

of Fame

nine patents

of IBM's

original P.C.'s

Dr. Dean holds three.

Thanks to Dr. Dean's

Microcomputer system

With bus control

for computer

attachments such as

disk drives,

video gear,

speakers,

scanners,

for growth

in information

technology means.

Sources

Ebony. "Modern Black Inventors". Chicago: John Publishing Co., 1988, p. 160.

Ebony. "Celebrating 100 Years of Excellence in Science". Chicago: Johnson Publishing Co., December 1999, p. 91.

Jet. "National Report: Modern Black Inventors". February 04, 2002, p. 16.

U.S. Patent Office Microfilm. *Mark Dean*. No, 4,528,626. July 9, 1985. U.S. Patent and Trademark Center. Detroit Public Library. Detroit, Michigan.

Ronald S. Demon

Cambridge, Massachusetts
Inventor- "Smart Shoe" - 1998
Senior Electrical Engineering Student MIT

Ronald Demon at sixteen
    had already seen
    that aching feet
    and basketball compete.

He pondered for days
    to find some ways
    to play basketball
    with no pain at all.

So, with computer knowledge,
    while a senior in college,
    he invents a "smart shoe"
    that knows what to do.

It adjusts to the wearer,
    the foot pain declarer.
It's a boon to podiatry
    and the sports society.

351

Sources

http://www.exodusnews.com/NATIONAL/.national03

http:web.mit.edu/invent/www/.inventorsA-H/de

"MIT Senior Issued Patent for 'Smart Shot'. *Jet*, November 23, 1998, p. 32.

U.S. Patent Office Microfilm. *Ronald S. Demon*. No. 5,813,142. September 29, 1998. Great Lakes Patent and Trademark Center. Detroit Public Library. Detroit, Michigan.

Dr. Philip Emeagwali

b. 1954; Nigeria

Research Scientist; St. Paul, Minnesota;

Inventor of the World's Fastest Computer

Dr. Emeagwali had an idea;
    to him it was very clear
that bees planned and constructed
    honeycombs that can't be obstructed
by inefficiency. So, he thought
    a computer made that way ought
to be powerful, efficient, fast.
    It was and better that the past!

His 65,000 processors fit a design,
    you might say, that bees would divine.
3.1 billions per second calculations!
    To the Doctor citations and acclamations!
His world's fastest computer now
    predicts the weather's when, and how.
We'll know of future global warming
    and when and where the earth is storming

Dr. Phillip, how does he do this?
    Wouldn't it be intellectual bliss

to have a similar needed skill

and be the first person to fill

a world wide technological need!

Father helped Dr. Phillip to succeed.

Father's decision when Phillip was age

nine was worthy of a genius or sage.

His decision- Phillip would every day

solve 100 math problems – no work, no play.

Today Phillip believes the daily drills

increased his mediocre math skills.

We should salute his father's decision

that shaped a mind for creative precision.

Father Emeagwali was a visionary

who understood the "necessary".

1989, for Phillip was the year,

the outstanding year, of his career.

He won the Gordon Bell Prize, known

as the Nobel of computing. A milestone

his supercomputer invention, helps the field

of petroleum with a better gas yield

and will eventually lower gas costs

thus less unrecovered gasoline losts.

Dr. Emeagwali's computer invention

    may some day mean more attention,

power, for personal computer users

    with more options and more choosers.

He is husband, father, achiever

    research scientist, modern believer

in technology, and the need for more

    young students to open the computing door.

Sources

Brown, Martha. *Upscale Magazine*. 1996.
http://emeagwali.com/African-american/upscale/African-american-inventors.html

Black Inventions Museum. *Interview*.
http://www.emeagwali.com/interviewsws/black-inventions/museum/African-american-inventors.html

Henderson, Ashyia N., editor. *Contemporary Black Biography*. (Detroit: Gale Group 2002, vol. 30), p. 61-63.

Henderson, Susan K. *African American Inventors, III*. (Mankato, MN: Capstone Press, 1998), p. 14-21.

Matney, William C., editor. *Who's Who Among Black Americans*. (Lake Forest, Illinois: Educational Communications, Inc., 1985), p. 446.

Wina Marché

Athan Gibbs, Sr.

Nashville, Tennessee;
Tennessee State University;
Tax Auditor State of Tennessee;
Invented a Voting Machine

Sometimes when we exercise
    a given right it would be wise
to have a way to simplify
    the system so folks don't lie
and take away any rights
    in dishonest political fights.

Now Athan Gibbs just might
    have the answer to right
the wrongs of ballot counting
    that keep common distrust mounting.
He has a foolproof voting machine
    that keeps the process simple and clean.

Gibbs' Tru Voter Validation
    System is an easy operation.
Just touch its t.v. screen
    to choose the candidate you mean

to win the specific election.

It operates with honest protection.

Put clearly, this is the news;

the candidate's picture you choose

by touching the picture on the t.v.

gets your vote as an electee.

Then you get a voting receipt;

no reading, no writing; it can't be beat!

Sources

http://www.dmreview.com/master.cfm?NavID=55&E

http://www.legislature.state.tn.us/bills/Prev

http://www.oakridger.com/stories/090301/stt-O

"Black Inventor Previews His Computer Voting System On Capitol Hill in Washington, D.C. *Jet*. July 30, 2001 v 100i7, p. 39.

"Modern Black Inventors", *Jet*. February 04, 2002, p. 16.

U.S. Patent Application Publication. Application No. *09/827,231*. File Apr. 5, 2001.

Wina Marché

Dr. Betty Wright Harris

Inventor-TATB (Explosive) Detector;
Los Alamos National Laboratory in New Mexico Operated by the
University of California for the United States Department of Energy

The spot test for TATB,
    for which Harris is the patentee
    allows for the explosive's testing
    when small amounts may be resting
    in areas of safety concern.
    Its presence is hard to confirm.

Dr. Harris has many awards
    for her family records.
She balances life between career
    and her four children, dear.
She promotes early encouragement
    for children with science intent.

Sources

Ebony. "Modern Black Inventors". October 1998, p. 160.

Sullivan, Otha Richard. Haskins, Jim, general editor. *Black Stars: African American Women Scientists and Inventors.* (New York: John Wiley & Sons, Inc., 2000), p. 83-87.

U.S. Patent Office Microfilm. *Betty Wright Harris.* No. 4,618,452. October 21, 1986. Great Lakes Patent and Trademark Center. Detroit Public Library. Detroit, Michigan.

Wina Marché

Michael J. Jackson

Los Angeles, California;
With Michael L. Bush and
Dennis Tompkins of Hollywood, California
Invented a Device for Anti-gravity Illusion

Michael J. Jackson, et al
    invented a device for defying
    gravity so Michael won't fall
    while dancing and trying
    a fancy foot move
    as he gets in the groove.
It made the book of patents U.S.
    as an anti-gravity process.

Source

U.S. Patent Office Microfilm. *Michael J. Jackson, et al.* No. 5,255,452. October 26, 1993. U.S. Great Lakes Patent & Trademark Center. Detroit Public Library. Detroit, Michigan.

Ruane Sharon Jeter

Industrial Engineer;
Inventor Six Medical Patents; Four Other Patents
Los Angeles, California

Inventor Ruane Jeter,
    is creative and productive,
    a ten times repeater
    with patents constructive.

Six for medical use
    with containers and such
    for waste and refuse-
    bearing the Jeter touch.

Another held by hand
    a multi-functional device-
    seven tools under command
    handy, useful, and precise.

For the home two,
    a pan with a special seal;
    and for a home menu
    a toaster for any meal.

Sources

Brown, Martha. *Upscale Magazine*. 1996.
http//:emeagwali.com/African-american/upscale/African-american-american-inventors.html

U.S. Patent Office Microfilm. *Ruane Sharon Jeter*. D289,249. April 14, 1987. Great Lakes Patent and Trademark Center. Detroit Public Library. Detroit, Michigan.

U.S. Patent Office Microfilm. *Ruane Sharon Jeter*. D383,783. September 16, 1997. Great Lakes Patent and Trademark Center. Detroit Public Library. Detroit, Michigan.

U.S. Patent Office Microfilm. *Ruane Sharon Jeter*. No. 5,947,285. September 7, 1999. Great Lakes Patent and Trademark Center. Detroit Public Library. Detroit, Michigan.

U.S. Patent Office Microfilm. *Ruane Sharon Jeter*. No. 5,918,762. July 6, 1999. Great Lakes Patent and Trademark Center. Detroit Public Library. Detroit, Michigan.

Lonnie G. Johnson

Smyrna, Georgia;

NASA Mechanical and Nuclear Engineer;

Inventor of the "Supersoaker" Squirt Gun

It was a chance observation;
    a water nozzle on a sink.
For Johnson it was a revelation
    that made him stop and think
    about the strong water spout
    that shot a blast of water out.

He is a jet propulsion engineer
    with several degrees from Tuskegee
    and the experience of a NASA career.
    Johnson's creative mind began to see
    the potential of the water's force
    and the distance of the water's course.

It's history, you know the rest,
    a toy pressurized water gun.
He experimented and began to test.
    When the many tests were done
America had a new toy sensation
    the "SuperSoaker", his revelation!

Sources

Amran, Fred M.B. *African American Inventors*. (*Mankato, MN:* Capstone Press, 1996), p. 8-13.

"Modern Black Inventors". *Jet*, February 4, 2002, p. 16.

U.S. Patent Office Microfilm. *Lonnie G. Johnson*. No. *4,591,071.* 1989. Great Lakes Patent and Trademark Center. Detroit Public Library. Detroit, Michigan.

U.S. Patent Office Microfilm. *Lonnie G. Johnson*. No. 5,586,688. December 24, 1996. Great Lakes Patent and Trademark Center. Detroit Public Library. Detroit, Michigan.

U.S. Patent Office Microfilm. *Lonnie G. Johnson*. No. 5,709,199. January 20, 1998. Great Lakes Patent and Trademark Center. Detroit Public Library. Detroit, Michigan.

U.S. Patent Office Microfilm. *Lonnie G. Johnson*. No. 5,592,931. January 14, 1997. Great Lakes Patent and Trademark Center. Detroit Public Library. Detroit, Michigan.

He has over thirty patents including Hair Dryer Curlers Apparatus, Smoke Detecting Timer Controlled, and Wet Diaper Detector.

Other patents RE35,412   5,707,270   5,553,598   5,592,931
    5,596,978   5,653,216   5,549,497   5,711,324   5,724,955
    5,699,781   5,197,452

Michel F. Molaire

More Than 93 Patents;
Kodak Chemist Rochester, New York

Molaire, a native of Haiti
    has patents over 93.
Twenty-five are in the U.S.;
    sixty-eight have a foreign address.
A research associate chemist
    Molaire is high on Kodak's list.
A top, prolific Kodak patentee,
    he is in their Distinguished Inventor Gallery.

Sources

Ebony. October, 1998, p. 160.

U.S. Patent Office Microfilm. *Michel F. Molaire*. No. 6,020,097. February 1, 2000. U.S. Patent & Trademark Center. Detroit Public Library. Detroit, Michigan.

U.S. Patent Office Microfilm. *Michel F. Molaire*. No. 5,232,804. August 3, 1993. U.S. Patent & Trademark Center. Detroit Public Library. Detroit, Michigan.

U.S. Patent Office Microfilm. *Michel F. Molaire*. No. 5,733,695. March 31, 1998. U.S. Patent & Trademark Center. Detroit Public Library. Detroit, Michigan.

Wina Marché

Orlando Robinson

Detroit, Michigan
Inventor: Seat Belt Shifter Lock (SBSL) 1998

Driving his fiancée to work
    one morning he stopped
    for a red light; another
    driver didn't and crashed into
    Robinson's car. He lost a life,
    His fiancée, his future wife.

Locking seat belts was her habit;
    but that day she didn't
    remember to lock hers.
    Orlanda's life changed that day.
    An unbuckled belt; a light went out;
    his life focus turned about.

Changing his planned career
    safety concerns became clear.
    A safety tool was his quest.
    How to block a car's starting
    if seat belts are unlocked.
    He had many ideas put to test.

Robinson found the answer-

> his SBSL, Seat Belt Shifter Lock
>
> is the result of his safety quest.
>
> SBSL will save precious lives.
>
> It works with existing car parts.
>
> When belts are locked the car starts!

Sources

http://www.bchle.org/22mar92fl.pdf

www.bchle.org

Michigan Chronicle. "Tragedy inspires an invention that will save lives." October 11, 2001, p. 1A. Detroit, Michigan.

Wina Marché

Richard Saxton

Patent Issued in Indianapolis, Indiana;
Invention: Dispenser for Pay Telephone – 1981

Saxton's patented invention
  had a clear cut intention.
It was for personal hygiene
  when using a public machine.
In this case, tissue for a pay
  phone to wipe others' germs away!

Sources

Brodie, James Michael. *Created Equal: The Lives and Ideas of Black American Innovators*. (New York: William Morrow and Company, 1993.), p. 173.

U.S. Patent Office Microfilm. *Richard Saxton*. No. 4,392,028. July 5, 1983. U.S. Patent & Trademark Center. Detroit Public Library. Detroit, Michigan.

Morris L. Smith

Lawnside, New Jersey;

Invention- Chemically Treated Paper - 1989

Inventor Morris L. Smith
    was experimenting with
    paper chemically treated.
The experiment was repeated.
Smith has patents two
    for ideas that are new.

Sources

U.S. Patent Office Microfilm. *Morris L. Smith*. No. 4,882,221. November 21, 1989. U.S. Patent & Trademark Center. Detroit Public Library. Detroit.

U.S. Patent Office Microfilm. *Morris L. Smith*. No. 4,883,475. November 28, 1989. U.S. Patent & Trademark Center. Detroit Public Library. Detroit.

Lanny S. Smoot

Patents 1989 and 1990
Morristown, New Jersey
Invention- Improved Teleconferencing Terminal with Screen

Lanny Smoot has an ear
   for business far and near.
With his invention a meeting
   is as easy as a simple greeting.
Certain folk are called together.
   They confer, share, and never
   leave their office, home, or city
   while they meet as a committee.

Sources

http://inventors.about.com/library/weekly/aa0
http://historicaltextarchive.com/sections.php
U.S. Patent Office Microfilm. *Lanny S. Smoot.* No, 4,890,314. December 26, 1989. U.S. Patent & Trademark Center. Detroit Public Library. Detroit, Michigan.
U.S. Patent Office Microfilm. *Lanny S. Smoot.* No. 4,928,301. May 22, 1990. U.S. Patent & Trademark Center. Detroit Public Library. Detroit, Michigan.

Valerie Thomas

Assistant Chief of the Space Data Operations Office
at NASA-Goddard Space-
Flight Center (GSFC) – Greenbelt, Maryland;
Patent for Illusion Transmitter 1980

Valerie was full of wonder and curiosity.
    She got a library electronics book
    hoping tinkering Dad would agree
    to help with whatever she undertook.

For Valerie this was not to be;
    technology and things mathematic
    are not for little girls, you see;
    about that folk were emphatic!

Valerie paid that belief no mind,
    but she did one mistake make.
    Girls don't get in the same bind!
    Take all the math you can take!

Had she taken advanced math before
    entering Morgan State University;
    about math she would have known more;
    physics would not have been an adversity.

In 1980, Valerie's patent for an "Illusion
    Transmitter", for projecting images from far away,
    proved that math ought to be an inclusion
    in girls' learning in this modern day.

Valerie's knowledge and skill
    she uses in NASA projects,
    that require her type of creative will;
    love for electronics she never regrets.

So girls, be not afraid of technology
    like Valerie study whatever you like.
    You can excel in an "ology"
    just as well as Joe or Mike!

Sources

Hayden, Robert C. *9 African American Inventors*. New York: Twenty-First Century Books, 1992.

Henderson, Susan K. African *American Inventors III*. (Mantako, MN: Capstone Press, 1998), p. 29-33.

U.S. Patent Office Microfilm. *Valerie Thomas*. Patent Number 4,229,761. October 21, 1980.

Dennis Weatherby

Inventor – Lemon Formula for Cascade Detergent;
Chemical Engineer for Proctor and Gamble

Chemical engineer Dennis Weatherby
    probably had no idea and didn't foresee
when he received his Masters degree
    that he would be a detergent patentee.

A dishwasher detergent automatic
    has some housewives and others ecstatic
about the spotless, sparkle, and shine
    that make their glassware look so fine!

So, it is for Proctor and Gamble
    that we write the following preamble;
"Let it be written for all to see
    Cascade's lemon formula was invented by Dennis Weatherby!"

Sources

Bellis, Mary. "Point to Ponder- Colors of Innovation – African
    American Innovators"

http://inventors.about.com/library/inventors/blkidprimer6_12aa.ht m

Ebony. "Modern Black Inventors". Johnson Publishing Co., October, 1998, p. 158.

U.S. Patent Office Microfilm. *Dennis Weatherby*. No. 4,714,562. December 22, 1985. U.S. Patent and Trademark Center. Detroit Public Library. Detroit, Michigan.

Dr. James West

Prince Edward County, Virginia (1931);
Acoustical Engineer;
Invention: Foil Electric Microphone;
Co-inventor with German Native, Gerhard M. Sessler;
Over 247 Patents

Dr. James West's name
    is a part of the National
    Inventors Hall of Fame.
His invention improves sound
    through voice microphones.
He and another co-found
    foil electric transdiscs
    for sound recording and voice
    providing more industry choice.

Dr. West is a patentee
    at least two hundred
    forty-seven times. You can see
    his co-invented device
    is now produced commercially
    at a reasonable price.
Inventor of the Year
    New Jersey – 1995
    West, their hometown engineer.

375

High esteem is for Dr. James West

    by folk professional and other wise

who consider him and his work the best!

    This they support with awards;

like *The Callinan Award* (The Electric Society of America)

Switch and Socket Award (National Patent Law Association)

AT&T Patent George R. Stibitz Trophy

The Silver Medal in Engineering Acoustics Award;

The Golden Torch Award (National Society of Black Engineers).

1998 Industrial Research Institute Achievement Award

Dr. James West, the inventor, the awards say he's the best!

    West, the writer, the Acoustical Society of America

an early work did attest that West was the best!

    His invention has had a great impact

on the U.S., abroad, on the world, in fact!

    Dr. West is husband, father, a person you would

love to have in your neighborhood!

Sources

"Engineer James West Inducted to National Inventors Hall of Fame in Akron, Ohio." *Jet*, Chicago: Johnson Publishing Co., July 27, 1999. p. 20.

"Dupont Presents 100 Years of Blacks in Science." *Ebony*. Chicago: Johnson Publishing Co., December 1999. p. 85-91.

"Bell Labs: James West Receives IRI's Achievement Award". http://www.bell-labs.com/news1998/october26/1.html

U.S. Patent Office Microfilm. *James West*. No. 3,945,112. March 23, 1976. U.S. Great Lakes Patent & Trademark Center. Detroit Public Library. Detroit, Michigan.

U.S. Patent Office Microfilm. *James West*. No. 4,248,808. February 3, 1981. U.S. Great Lakes Patent & Trademark Center. Detroit Public Library. Detroit, Michigan.

U.S. Patent Office Microfilm. *James West*. No. 4,802,227. January 31, 1989. U.S. Great Lakes Patent & Trademark Center. Detroit Public Library. Detroit, Michigan.

Appendix

More African American Patent Holders in Science, Medicine, and Technology
U.S. Patent Numbers

Adams, James S.

Propelling means for aeroplanes. *1,356,329*. Oct. 19, 1920

Ancker Johnson, Betsy

Signal generators. *3,287,659*. Nov. 22, 1966

Asom, Moses, T.

Semiconductor device based on optical transitions between quasibound

Energy levels. *5,386,126*. July 31, 1995

Baron, Neville A.

Apparatus and process for recurving the cornea of the eye. *4,461,294*.

July 24, 1984

Bauer, James A.

Coin changer mechanism. *3,490,571*. Jan. 20, 1971

Benton, James

Level-derrick. *658,939.* Oct. 2, 1990. Walked over 700 miles from Kentucky to

Washington, D.C. carrying his invention to get a patent.

Blair, Henry

Farm implements. – Seed Planter. *8447X.*

Second known African American patent holder. Held three patents.

Boone, Sarah

An ironing board. *473,653.* Apr. 26, 1892.

Bradberry, Henrietta

Underwater torpedo discharge means (cannon). *2,390,688.* Dec. 11, 1945

Brooks, Phil.

Disposable syringe. *3,802,434.* Apr. 9, 1974

Brown, Firmin Charles

Self-feeding attachment for furnaces. *1,719,258.* July 2, 1929

Brown, Henry T.

Reactivating hydroforming catalysts. Oct. 22, 1968

More African American Patent Holders in Science, Medicine, and Technology

Brown, Marie Van Brittan

Home security system. *3,482,037*. Dec. 2, 1969

Cadet, Gardy

Acoustic analysis of gas. *5,948,967*. Sept. 7, 1999

Other patents between 1991 and 1999

5,427,659   *5,501,098*   *5,510,007*   *5,625,140*

5,474,659   *5,877,407*   *5,392,635*

Cassell, Oscar Robert

A flying machine. *1,024,766*. Apr. 30, 1912; *1,406,344*. Feb. 14, 1922

Christine, John B.

Many patents in chemical engineering

Grease composition for high temperature and high speeds. *3,518,189*. June 30, 1970

Cooper, James

Elevator safety device. *536,605*. Apr. 2, 1895

Cooper, John Richard

Process for isolating a fluorine-containing polymer. *3,536,683.*
Oct. 27, 1970

Cosby, Thomas L.

Closed cycle energy conversion system. *3,826,092.* July 30, 1974

Cosgrove, William Francis

Automatic stop plug for for gas and oil pipes. *313,993.* Mar. 17,
1885

Cotton, Donald J.

Capillary liquid fuel nuclear reactor. *4,327,443.* Apr. 27, 1982

Creamer, Henry

Steam feed-water trap. *376,586.* Jan. 17, 1888

Dacons, Joseph Carl

Process for manufacturing nitroform and its salts. *3,125,606.* Mar.
17, 1964

He has numerous patents in organic chemistry.

Davis, Stephen H.

Load weighing and totaling device for cranes, hoists and the like.
2,324,769.

July 20, 1943

Dent, Anthony L.

Rehydrated Silica gel dentrifrice abrasive. *4,346,071*. Aug. 24, 1982

Dickinson, Joseph Hunter

A phonograph; a player-piano; a reed-organ. *1,252,411*. Jan. 8, 1918

1,028,996. June 11, 1912; *624,192*. May 2, 1899.

Dorman, Linneaus Cuthbert

Absorbents for airborne formaldehyde. *4,517,111*. May 14, 1985

Downing, Phillip

Street railway switch. *430,118*. June 17, 1890

Dugger, Cortland Otis

"Duggerite" – barium magnesium aluminate. Method for growing single oxide

crystals. *3,595,803*. July 27, 1971

Emile, Philip E.

Transistorized gating system. *2,982,868*. May 2, 1961

Frye, Clara E.

Surgical appliance. *847,758*. March 19, 1907

Garner, Albert Y.

Flame retardant. *3,989,702*. Nov. 2, 1976

Gaskin, Frances C.

Sun protectant composition and method. *4,806,344*. Feb. 21, 1989

Hall, Lloyd A.

Food chemist. Has over 100 patents. Meat-curing composition. *2,770,551*. Nov. 13, 1956

Harper, Solomon

Thermostatic controlled fur and material dressing equipment. *2,711,095*. June 21, 1955

Harrison, Emmett Scott

Turbojet afterburner engine with two-position exhaust nozzle. *4,242,865*. Jan. 6, 1981

Hull, Wilson E.

Mass release mechanism for satellites. *3,424,403*. Jan. 28, 1969

Jackson, William H.

Railway switch. *578,641*. Mar. 9, 1897

Jennings, Thomas L.

> Dry cleaning process. *3306X*. Mar. 3, 1821
>
>> First known African American to receive a U.S. patent.

Johnson, John Arthur "Jack"

> Wrench. *1,413,121*. Apr. 18, 1922
>
>> Theft-preventing device for vehicles. *1,438,709*. Dec. 22, 1922
>>
>> First African American Heavy weight champion of the world.

Jones, Frederick McKinley

> Air conditioning unit. *2,475,841*. July 12, 1949
>
>> His inventions made it possible to refrigerate trucks. His patents include many refrigeration and cooling devices, ticket dispensers; internal combustion engine; a starter generator; two-cycle gas engine. He was a "virtual inventing machine"!

Jones, Howard St. Claire, Jr.

> Electronically scanned microwave antennas. *3,268,901*. Aug. 23, 1966
>
>> He has many patents in the area of microwaves and antennas.

Jones, William B.

> Dentist apparatus. *2,096,375*. Oct. 19, 1937

Joyner, Marjorie Stewart

Permanent waving machine. *1,693,515.* Nov. 27, 1928

Julian, Hubert

Air safety appliance. *1,379,264*

Kenner, Beatrice

Personal and health care device. *4,696,068.* Sept. 29, 1987. She
has five patents.

Knox, William J. Jr.

Coating aids for photographic elements. *3,539,352.* Nov. 10, 1970

He has numerous patents for photography related processes.

Latimer, Lewis Howard

Process for manufacturing carbons. *252,386.* Jan. 17, 1882

Latimer was one of the "Edison Pioneers" with patents in
electricity.

Lavalette, William A.

Improved printing press. *208,184.* Sept. 17, 1878

Lee, Joseph

Automatic bread making machine. *524,042.* Aug. 7, 1894

LeVert, Francis Edward

Threshold self-powered gamma detector for use as a monitor of power in a nuclear reactor. *4,091,288*. May 23, 1978. He has numerous physics related patents.

Lewis, James Earl

Antenna feed for two coordinate tracking radars. *3,388,399*. June 11, 1968

MacDonald, Hugh D., Jr.

Rocket catapult. *3,447,767*. June 3, 1969

Madison, Shannon L.

Electrical wiring harness termination systems. *4,793,820*. Dec. 27, 1988

Maloney, Kenneth Morgan

Alumina coatings for mercury vapor lamps. *4,079,288*. Mar. 14, 1978

Matzeliger, Jan Earnst

Shoe lasting machine. *274,207*. Mar. 20, 1882.

Shoe lasting machine. *459,899*. Sept. 22, 1891

He revolutionized shoe making.

Until his invention shoes were finished by hand.

McClennan, Walter N.

An automatic railway car door. *1,333,430*. Mar. 9, 1920

McCoy, Elijah

Oil cup. A device that allows lubricating while vehicle is in motion.

614,307. Nov. 15, 1898. McCoy is the "real McCoy". He had over twenty patents for lubricators, as well as, patents for a lawn sprinkler, a medicine cup, a steam dome, and an ironing board for the home.

Millington, James E.

Method of making expandable styrene-type beads. *4,286,069*. Aug. 25, 1981

Morgan, Garrett Augustus

Breathing device (a gas mask). *1,113,675*. Oct. 13, 1914

Traffic signal. *1,475,024*. Nov. 20, 1923. The first traffic signal; it was three-way.

Neblett, Richard Flemon

Oil-soluble ashless disperant-detergent-inhibitors. *3,511,780*. May 12, 1970

Parker, Alice

A heating furnace. *1,325,905*. Dec. 23, 1919

Rillieux, Norbert

> Sugar process. *3,237*. Aug. 26, 1843
>> Rillieux revolutionized the sugar industry.

Robinson, Elbert R.

> Grooved railway wheel. *594,286*. Nov. 23, 1897
>> Electric railway trolley. *594,286*. Sept. 19, 1893
>>> Two large corporations stole his ideas. The Supreme Court
>>> ruled in his favor in one case to the tune of

$31,000,000!

Russell, Edwin R.

> The separation of plutonium from uranium and fission products.
> *2,855,269*.
>> Oct. 7, 1958

Ryder, Earl

> High silicon cast iron. *3,129,095*. Apr. 14, 1964

Samms, Adolphus

> Rocket engine pump feed system. *3,000,179*. Sept. 19, 1961
>> Multiple stage rocket. *3,199,455*. Aug. 10, 1965
>>> Emergency release for extraction chute. *3,257,089*. June
>>> 21, 1966
>>>> Rocket motor fuel feed. *3,310,936*. March 28, 1967

Sampson, Henry Thomas

Binder system for propellants and explosives. *3,140,210*. July 7, 1964

Gamma electric cell. *3,591,860*. July 28, 1970

Sanderson, Dewey S.C.

Urinalysis machine. *3,522,011*. July 28, 1970

Sanderson, Ralph W.

Hydraulic shock absorber. *3,362,742*. Jan. 9, 1968

Shaw, Earl D.

Free-electron amplifier device with electromagnetic radiation delay element

4,529,942. July 16, 1985

Stewart, Albert Clifton

Electric cell. *3,25,045*. June 7, 1966

Weir, Charles E.

High pressure optical cell. *3,079,505*. Feb. 26, 1963

Williams, Paul E.

A helicopter. *3,065,933*. Nov. 27, 1962

Woods, Granville T.

    Third rail for electrified railways. *463,020.* Nov. 10, 1891

        Granville has been called "the greatest inventor in the world".

        He has more than fifty patents.

        Some of them are;

            A steam boiler furnace

            An electro-mechanical brake

            A train for an amusement park

            System of electrical distribution

            Automatic safety cutout switch circuits

            An improved phonograph

            Electromagnetic brakes

            Railway telegraphy

            Electric egg incubator

Index

About the Author

A versatile educator Wina Marché has taught young learners and adults in the following education systems: Detroit's Wayne County Community College District, Detroit Public Schools-elementary, and the United States Government Overseas Education System-France. Before becoming an educator Wina Marché was a newspaper reporter/columnist and later a social worker.

She has received numerous awards for community service and academic excellence. Her Undergraduate and Masters degrees are from Wayne State University. Her doctorate in Higher Education Administration is from the University of Michigan.

Her first book, *The Poetry of African American Invention: When One Door Closes Another Opens,* is about inventors and their inventions. She is currently working on two manuscripts for children, *I Love Books!* and *Thoughts and Such.*

Printed in the United States
37945LVS00005B/35